Frances Lawton

The Dream

THE POEMS OF THE HON. MRS. NORTON,

WITH

A NOTICE OF THE AUTHOR

BY

RUFUS W. GRISWOLD

NEW YORK:
LEAVITT & ALLEN,
379 BROADWAY
1856.

CONTENTS.

MEMOIR OF MRS. NORTON.

The women of England have in the present century produced more good poetry than in all previous ages. Mrs. Tighe, Joanna Baillie, Mrs. Hemans, Elizabeth B. Barret, Miss Landon, and Mrs. Norton are worthy to be ranked with almost any half dozen contemporaries of the other sex.

Mrs. Norton has been styled "the female Byron." She resembles the greatest poet of modern times in all but his vices. Like the noble bard she was ill-mated in her marriage Her mind has been fashioned by misfortune Her poetry mirrors her feelings. It is, what some critics have contended all poetry should be, "the lyrical expression of passion."

Caroline Elizabeth Sarah Norton is the grand-daughter of Richard Brinsley Sheridan, and the inheritor of his genius. While she was an infant her father sought the renovation of a shattered constitution in the southern seas. He died at the Cape of Good Hope, four or five years after leaving England, and his young and beautiful widow returned, to devote herself with untiring assiduity to the education of her children, the subject of this notice and a sister, now the wife of the Hon. Price Blackwood.

These sisters exhibited an almost unexampled precocity. They rivalled the celebrated Misses Davidson of this country in the earliness and perfection of their mental developement. At twelve Caroline Sheridan wrote verses which even now she would not be ashamed to see in print, and at seventeen she finished "The Sorrows of Rosalie," which gave abundant promise of the reputation she has since acquired.

Two years afterward she was married to the Hon. George Chapple Norton, a brother to Lord Grantley. We have spoken of her marriage as unfortunate. Hemans, Tighe, Landon and Norton! how strange that all the great poetesses of England who wedded at all should have wedded so unhappily! Mr. Norton proposed for Miss Sheridan when she was sixteen; but her mother postponed the contract three years, that the daughter might herself be better quali fied to fix her choice. In this period she became acquainted with one whose early death alone prevented a union more consonant to her feelings, and at nineteen she accepted the hand of Mr. Norton—a man of a lower range of feelings, whose only nobility was in his blood. The marriage, as might have been anticipated, was an unblessed one. Yet they lived years together—he not quite insensible to the honor of being the husband of the first woman in the empire, and she duteously enduring the indifference and neglect of a man who could appreciate her only as the public praised. At length, incited by the political enemies of Lord Melbourne, then Prime Minister, he commenced legal proceedings against that nobleman, on a charge involving her infidelity. All the low arts which well-feed attorneys and a malignant prosecutor could devise were put in requisition. Forgery, perjury, the searching scrutiny of private papers, the exhibition of all the most thoughtless and trivial incidents and conversations in the history of a "woman of genius living in the world," were unavailing. She passed the ordeal with her white robes unsullied by the slightest stain. But an acquittal by the jury and the people poorly atoned the injustice of the base accusation.

Mrs. Norton now lives in comparative retirement. She is still one of the most beautiful women of England. Mr. Willis, in his "Lady Jane," thus described her, three years ago,—

She had a low, sweet brow, with fringed lakes
  Of an unfathom'd darkness couch'd below;
And parted on that brow in jetty flakes
  The raven hair swept back with wavy flow,
Rounding a head of such a shape as makes
  The old Greek marble with the goddess glow
Her nostril's breaching arch might threaten storm—
But love lay in her lips, all hush'd and warm.

And small teeth, glittering white, and cheek whose reu
  Seem'd Passion, there asleep, in rosy nest:
And neck set on as if to bear a head—
  May be a lily, may be Juno's crest,—
So lightly sprang it from its snow-white bed!
  So proudly rode above the swelling breast!
And motion, effortless as stars awaking
And melting out, at eve, and morning's breaking;

And voice delicious quite, and smile that came
  Slow to the lips, as 'twere the heart smiled through
These charms I've been particular to name,
  For they are, like an inventory, true,

And of themselves were stuff enough for fame;
 But she, so wondrous fair, has genius too,
And brilliantly her thread of life is spun—
In verse and beauty both, the "Undying One!"

And song—for in those kindling lips there lay
 Music to wing all utterance outward breaking,
As if upon the ivory teeth did play
 Angels, who caught the words at their awaking,
And sped them with sweet melodies away—
 The hearts of those who listen'd with them taking.

The poetry of Mrs. Norton is often distinguished for a masculine energy, and always for grace and harmony. She has published three volumes, "The Sorrows of Rosalie," "The Undying One," and "The Dream and other Poems." The last, and the better portions of the first and second, are included in the present publication

TO

THE DUCHESS OF SUTHERLAND.

ONCE more, my harp! once more, although I thought
Never to wake thy silent strings again,
A soothing dream thy gentle chords have wrought
And my sad heart, which long hath dwelt in pain,
Soars, like a wild bird from a cypress bough,
Into the Poet's Heaven, and leaves dull grief below!

And unto Thee—the beautiful and pure—
Whose lot is cast amid that busy world
Where only sluggish Dulness dwells secure,
And Fancy's generous wing is faintly furl'd;
To thee—whose friendship kept its equal truth
Through the most dreary hour of my embitter'd youth—

I dedicate the lay. Ah! never bard,
In days when Poverty was twin with song;
Nor wandering harper, lonely and ill-starr'd,
Cheer'd by some castle's chief, and harbor'd long;
Not Scott's "Last Minstrel," in his trembling lays,
Woke with a warmer heart the earnest meed of praise!

For easy are the alms the rich man spares
To sons of Genius, by misfortune bent
But thou gav'st *me*, what woman seldom dares,
Belief—in spite of many a cold dissent—

When, slandered and maligned, I stood apart,
From those whose bounded power, hath wrung, not
crushed, my heart.

Then, then, when cowards lied away my name,
And scoff'd to see me feebly stem the tide;
When some were kind on whom I had no claim,
And some forsook on whom my love relied,
And some, who *might* have battled for my sake,
Stood off in doubt to see what turn "the world" would
take—

Thou gavest me that the poor do give the poor,
Kind words, and holy wishes, and true tears;
The loved, the near of kin, could do no more,
Who changed not with the gloom of varying years,
But clung the closer when I stood forlorn,
And blunted Slander's dart with their indignant scorn.

For they who credit crime are they who feel
Their *own* hearts weak to unresisted sin; [steal
Mem'ry, not judgment, prompts the thoughts which
O'er minds like these, an easy faith to win;
And tales of broken truth are still believed
Most readily by those who have *themselves* deceived.

But, like a white swan down a troubled stream,
Whose ruffling pinion hath the power to fling
Aside the turbid drops which darkly gleam
And mar the freshness of her snowy wing,
So Thou, with queenly grace and gentle pride,
Along the world's dark waves in purity dost glide;

Thy pale and pearly cheek was never made
  To crimson with a faint false-hearted shame:
Thou didst not shrink,—of bitter tongues afraid,
  Who hunt in packs the object of their blame;
To Thee the sad denial still held true,
For from thine own good thoughts thy heart its mercy drew

And, though my faint and tributary rhymes
  Add nothing to the glory of thy day,
Yet every Poet *hopes* that after-times
  Shall set some value on his votive lay,—
And I would fain one gentle deed record
Among the many such with which thy life is stored.

So, when these lines, made in a mournful hour,
  Are idly open'd to the Stranger's eye,
A dream of THEE, aroused by Fancy's power,
  Shall be the first to wander floating by;
And they who never saw thy lovely face,
Shall pause,—to conjure up a vision of its grace!

THE DREAM.

'Twas summer eve; the changeful beams still play'd
On the fir-bark and through the beechen shade;
Still with soft crimson glow'd each floating cloud,
Still the stream glitter'd where the willow bow'd;
Still the pale moon sate silent and alone,
Nor yet the stars had rallied round her throne;
Those diamond courtiers, who, while yet the West
Wears the red shield above his dying breast,
Dare not assume the loss they all desire,
Nor pay their homage to the fainter fire,
But wait in trembling till the Sun's fair light
Fading, shall leave them free to welcome night!

So when some Chief, whose name through realms afar
Was still the watchword of successful war,
Met by the fatal hour which waits for all,
Is, on the field he rallied, forced to fall,
The conquerors pause to watch his parting breath,
Awed by the terrors of that mighty death:

Nor dared the meed of victory to claim,
Nor lift the standard to a meaner name,
Till every spark of soul hath ebb'd away,
And leaves what was a hero, common clay.

Oh! Twilight! Spirit that dost render birth
To dim enchantments; melting Heaven with Earth,
Leaving on craggy hills and running streams
A softness like the atmosphere of dreams;
Thy hour to all is welcome! Faint and sweet
Thy light falls round the peasant's homeward feet,
Who, slow returning from his task of toil,
Sees the low sunset gild the cultured soil,
And, tho' such radiance round him brightly glows,
Marks the small spark his cottage window throws.
Still as his heart forestals his weary pace,
Fondly he dreams of each familiar face,
Recalls the treasures of his narrow life,
His rosy children, and his sunburnt wife,
To whom *his* coming is the chief event
Of simple days in cheerful labor spent.
The rich man's chariot hath gone whirling past,
And those poor cottagers have only cast
One careless glance on all that show of pride,
Then to their tasks turn'd quietly aside;
But *him* they wait for, him they welcome home,
Fond sentinels look forth to see him come;
The fagot sent for when the fire grew dim,

The frugal meal prepared, are all for him;
For him the watching of that sturdy boy
For him those smiles of tenderness and joy,
For him.—who plods his sauntering way along,
Whistling the fragment of some village song!

Dear art thou to the lover, thou sweet light,
Fair fleeting sister of the mournful night!
As in impatient hope he stands apart,
Companion'd only by his beating heart,
And with an eager fancy oft beholds
The vision of a white robe's fluttering folds
Flit through the grove, and gain the open mead,
True to the hour by loving hearts agreed!
At length she comes. The evening's holy grace
Mellows the glory of her radiant face;
The curtain of that daylight faint and pale
Hangs round her like the shrouding of a veil;
As, turning with a bashful timid thought,
From the dear welcome she herself hath sought
Her shadowy profile drawn against the sky
Cheats, while it charms, his fond adoring eye.

Oh! dear to him, to all, since first the flowers
Of happy Eden's consecrated bowers
Heard the low breeze along the branches play,
And God's voice bless the cool hour of the day.
For though that glorious Paradise be lost,
Though earth by blighting storms be roughly cross'd,
Though the long curse demands the tax of sin,
And the day's sorrows with the day begin,

That hour, once sacred to God's presence, still
Keeps itself calmer from the touch of ill,
The holiest hour of Earth. *Then* toil doth cease—
Then from the yoke the oxen find release—
Then man rests pausing from his many cares,
And the world teems with children's sunset prayers!
Then innocent things seek out their natural rest,
The babe sinks slumbering on its mother's breast;
The birds beneath their leafy covering creep,
Yea, even the flowers fold up their buds in sleep,
And angels, floating by, on radiant wings,
Hear the low sound the breeze of evening brings,
Catch the sweet incense as it floats along,
The infant's prayer, the mother's cradle-song,
And bear the holy gifts to worlds afar,
As things too sacred for this fallen star.

At such an hour, on such a summer night,
Silent and calm in its transparent light,
A widow'd parent watch'd her slumbering child,
On whose young face the sixteenth summer smiled.
Fair was the face she watch'd! Nor less, because
Beauty's perfection seemed to make a pause,
And wait, on that smooth brow, some further touch,
Some spell from time,—the great magician,—such

As calls the closed bud out of hidden gloom,
And bids it wake to glory, light, and bloom.
Girlish as yet, but with the gentle grace
Of a young fawn in its low resting-place,
Her folded limbs were lying: from her hand
A group of wild flowers—Nature's brightest band,
Of all that laugh along the summer fields,
Of all the sunny hedge-row freely yields,
Of all that in the wild-wood darkly hide,
Or on the thyme-bank wave in breezy pride,—
Show'd that the weariness which closed in sleep
So tranquil, child-like, innocent, and deep,
Nor festal gaiety, nor toilsome hours,
Had brought; but, like a flower among the flowers,
She had been wandering 'neath a summer sky,
Youth on her lip and gladness in her eye,
Twisting the wild rose from its native thorn,
And the blue scabious from the sunny corn;
Smiling and singing like a spirit fair
That walk'd the world, but had no dwelling there.
And still (as though their faintly-scented breath
Preserv'd a meek fidelity in death)
Each late imprison'd blossom fondly lingers
Within the touch of her unconscious fingers,
Though, languidly unclasp'd, that hand no more
Guards its possession of the rifled store.

So wearily she lay; so sweetly slept;
So by her side fond watch the mother kept;

And, as above her gentle child she bent,
So like they seem'd in form and lineament,
You might have deem'd her face its shadow gave
To the clear mirror of a fountain's wave;
Only in this they differ'd; that, while one
Was warm and radiant as the summer sun,
The other's smile had more a moonlight play
For many tears had wept its glow away;
Yet was she fair; of loveliness so true,
That time, which faded, never could subdue;
And though the sleeper, like a half-blown rose
Show'd bright as angels in her soft repose,
Though bluer veins ran through each snowy lid,
Curtaining sweet eyes, by long dark lashes hid—
Eyes that as yet had never learnt to weep,
But woke up smiling, like a child's, from sleep;—
Though fainter lines were pencill'd on the brow,
Which cast soft shadow on the orbs below;
Though deeper color flush'd her youthful cheek,
In its smooth curve more joyous and less meek,
And fuller seem'd the small and crimson mouth,
With teeth like those that glitter in the south—
She had but youth's superior brightness, such
As the skill'd painter gives with flattering touch
When he would picture every lingering grace
Which once shone brighter in some copied face;
And it was compliment, whene'er she smiled,
To say, "Thou'rt like thy mother, my fair child!"

Sweet is the image of the brooding dove!—
Holy as Heaven a mother's tender love!
The love of many prayers and many tears,
Which changes not with dim declining years—
The *only* love which on this teeming earth
Asks no return from Passion's wayward birth;
The only love that, with a touch divine,
Displaces from the heart's most secret shrine
The idol SELF. Oh! prized beneath thy due
When life's untried affections all are new—
Love, from whose calmer hope and holier rest
(Like a fledged bird, impatient of the nest)
The human heart, rebellious, springs to seek
Delights more vehement, in ties more weak;
How strange to us appears, in after-life,
That term of mingled carelessness and strife,
When guardianship so gentle gall'd our pride,
When it was holiday to leave thy side,
When, with dull ignorance that *would not* learn,
We lost those hours that never can return—
Hours, whose most sweet communion Nature meant
Should be in confidence and kindness spent,
That we (hereafter mourning) might believe
In human faith, though all around deceive;
Might weigh against the sad and startling crowd
Of ills which wound the weak and chill the proud,
Of woes 'neath which (despite of stubborn will,
Philosophy's vain boast, and erring skill)
The strong heart downward like a willow bends,
Failure of love,—and treachery of friends,—
Our recollections of the undefiled,

The sainted tie, of parent and of child!
Oh! happy days! Oh years that glided by,
Scarce chronicled by one poor passing sigh!
When the dark storm sweeps past us, and the soul
Struggles with fainting strength to reach the goal;
When the false baits that lured us only cloy,
What would we give to grasp your vanish'd joy!
From the cold quicksands of Life's treacherous shore
The backward light our anxious eyes explore,
Measure the miles our wandering feet have come,
Sinking heart-weary, far away from home,
Recall the voice that whisper'd love and peace
The smile that bid our early sorrows cease,
And long to bow our grieving heads, and weep
Low on the gentle breast that lull'd us first to sleep!

Ah! bless'd are they for whom 'mid all their pains
That faithful and unalter'd love remains;
Who, Life wreck'd round them,—hunted from their rest,—
And, by all else forsaken or distress'd,—
Claim, in *one* heart, their sanctuary and shrine—
As I, my Mother, claim'd my place in thine!

Oft, since that hour, in sadness I retrace
My childhood's vision of thy calm sweet face•

Oft see thy form, its mournful beauty shrouded
  In thy black weeds, and coif of widow's woe;
Thy dark expressive eyes all dim and clouded
  By that deep wretchedness the lonely know:
Stifling thy grief, to hear some weary task
  Conn'd by unwilling lips, with listless air,
Hoarding thy means, lest future need might ask
  More than the widow's pittance then could spare.
Hidden, forgotten by the great and gay,
  Enduring sorrow, not by fits and starts,
But the long self-denial, day by day,
  Alone amidst thy brood of careless hearts!
Striving to guide, to teach, or to restrain,
  The young rebellious spirits crowding round,
Who saw not, knew not, felt not for thy pain,
  And could not comfort—yet had power to wound!
Ah! how my selfish heart, which since hath grown
Familiar with deep trials of its own,
With riper judgment looking to the past,
Regrets the careless days that flew so fast,
Stamps with remorse each wasted hour of time,
And darkens every folly into crime!

Warriors and statesmen have their meed of praise,
  And what they do or suffer men record;
But the long sacrifice of woman's days
  Passes without a thought—without a word;
And many a holy struggle for the sake

Of duties sternly, faithfully fulfill'd—
For which the anxious mind must watch and
wake,
And the strong feelings of the heart be
still'd,—
Goes by unheeded as the summer wind,
And leaves no memory and no trace behind!
Yet, it may be, more lofty courage dwells
In one meek heart which braves an adverse
fate,
Than his, whose ardent soul indignant swells
Warm'd by the fight, or cheer'd through high
debate:
The Soldier dies surrounded; could he *live*
Alone to suffer, and alone to strive?

Answer, ye graves, whose suicidal gloom
Shows deeper horror than a common tomb!
Who sleep within? The men who would evade
An unseen lot of which they felt afraid.
Embarrassment of means, which work'd an-
noy,—
A past remorse,—a future blank of joy,—
The sinful rashness of a blank despair,—
These were the strokes which sent your victims
there.

In many a village churchyard's simple grave,
Where all unmark'd the cypress branches wave
In many a vault where Death could only claim
The brief inscription of a woman's name;
Of different ranks, and different degrees,
From daily labor to a life of ease,

(From the rich wife who through the weary day
Wept in her jewels, grief's unceasing prey,
To the poor soul who trudged o'er marsh and moor,
And with her baby begg'd from door to door,—)
Lie hearts, which, ere they found that last release,
Had lost all memory of the blessing "Peace;"
Hearts, whose long struggle through unpitied years
None saw but Him who marks the mourner's tears;
The obscurely noble! who evaded not
The woe which He had will'd should be their lot,
But nerved themselves to bear!

Of such art thou,
My Mother! With thy calm and holy brow,
And high devoted heart, which suffer'd still
Unmurmuring, through each degree of ill.
And, because Fate hath will'd that mine should be
A Poet's soul (at least in my degree,)—
And that my verse would faintly shadow forth
What I have seen of pure unselfish worth,—
Therefore I speak of Thee; that those who read
That trust in woman, which is still my creed,
Thy early-widow'd image may recall
And greet thy nature as the type of all!

Enough! With eyes of fond unwearied love
The Mother of my story watch'd above

Her sleeping child ; and, as she views the grace
And blushing beauty of that girlish face,
Her thoughts roam back through change of time
and tide,
Since first Heaven sent the blessing by her side.

In that sweet vision she again receives
The snow-white cradle, where that tiny head
Lay, like a small bud folded in its leaves,
Foster'd with dew by tears of fondness shed ;
Each infantine event, each dangerous hour
Which pass'd with threatening o'er its fragile
form,
Her hope, her anguish, as the tender flower
Bloom'd to the sun, or sicken'd in the storm,
In memory's magic mirror glide along,
And scarce she notes the different scene
around,
And scarce her lips refrain the cradle-song
Which sooth'd that infant with its lulling
sound !
But the dream changes ; quiet years roll on ;
That dawn of frail existence fleets away,
And she beholds beneath the summer sun
A blessed sight ; a little child at play.
The soft light falls upon its golden hair,
And shows a brow intelligently mild ;
No more a cipher in this world of care,
Love cheers and chides that happy conscious
child.
No more unheeding of her watchful love,
Pride to excel, its docile spirit stirs ;

Regret and hope its tiny bosom move,
And looks of fondness brightly answer hers;
O'er the green meadow, and the broomy hill,
In restless joy it bounds and dārts along;
Or through the breath of evening, low and still,
Carols with mirthful voice its welcome song.

Again the vision changes; from her view
The CHILD's dear love and antic mirth are gone;
But, in their stead, with cheek of rose-leaf hue,
And fair slight form, and low and silvery tone,
Rises the sweetest spirit Thought can call
From memory's distant worlds—the fairy GIRL;
Whose heart her childish pleasures still enthrall,
Whose unbound hair still floats in careless curl,
But in whose blue and meekly lifted eyes,
And in whose shy, though sweet and cordial smile,
And in whose changeful blushes, dimly rise
Shadows and lights that were not seen erewhile:
Shadows and lights that speak of woman's love,
Of all that makes or mars her fate below;
Mysterious prophecies, which Time must prove
More bright in glory, or more dark with woe!
And that soft vision also wanders by,
Melting in fond and innocent smiles away,
Till the loved REAL meets the watchful eye
Of her who thus recall'd a former day;
The gentle daughter, for whose precious sake

Her widow'd heart had struggled with its pain,
And still through lonely grief refused to break,
Because *that* tie to Earth did yet remain.
Now, as she fondly gazed, a few meek tears
Stole down her cheek; for she that slumber'd there,
The beautiful, the loved of many years,
A bride betroth'd must leave her fostering care;
Woo'd in another's home apart to dwell—
Oh! might that other love but half as well!
As if the mournful wish had touch'd her heart,
The slumbering maiden woke, with sudden start;
Turn'd, with a dazzled and intense surprise,
On that fond face her bright, bewilder'd eyes;
Gazed round on each familiar object near,
As though she doubted yet if sense was clear,
Cover'd her brow and sigh'd, as though to wake
Had power some spell of happy thought to break;
Then murmur'd, in a low and earnest tone,
"Oh! is that blessed dream for ever gone?"

Strange is the power of dreams! Who hath not felt,
When in the light such visions melt,
How the veil'd soul, though struggling to be free,
Ruled by that deep unfathom'd mystery,
Wakes, haunted by the thoughts of good or ill,
Whose shadowy influence pursues us still?

Sometimes romorse doth weigh our spirits down;
Some crime committed earns Heaven's angriest frown;
Some awful sin, in which the tempted heart
Hath scarce, perhaps, forborne its waking part,
Brings dreams of judgment; loud the thunders roll,
The heavens shrink blacken'd like a flaming scroll;
We faint, we die, beneath the avenging rod,
And vainly hide from our offended God.
For oh! though fancy change our mortal lot,
And rule our slumbers, CONSCIENCE sleepeth not;
That strange sad dial, by its own true light,
Points to our thoughts, how dark soe'er the night,
Still by our pillow watchful guard it keeps,
And bids the sinner tremble while he sleeps.

Sometimes, with fearful dangers doom'd to cope,
'Reft of each wild and visionary hope,
Stabb'd with a thousand wounds, we struggle still,
The hand that tortures, powerless to kill.
Sometimes 'mid ocean storms, in fearful strife,
We stem the wave, and shrieking, gasp for life,
While crowding round us, faces rise and gleam,
Some known and loved, some, pictures of our dream

High on the buoyant waters wildly toss'd—
Low in its foaming caverns darkly lost—
Those flitting forms the dangerous hour partake,
Cling to our aid, or suffer for our sake.
Conscious of present life, the slumbering soul
Still floats us onward, as the billows roll,
Till, snatch'd from death, we seem to touch the strand,
Rise on the shoreward wave, and dash to land!
Alone we come: the forms whose wild array
Gleam'd round us while we struggled, fade away—
We know not, reck not, who the danger shared,
But, vaguely dreaming, feel that *we* are spared.

Sometimes a grief, of fond affection born,
Gnaws at our heart, and bids us weep till morn;
Some anguish, copied from our waking fears,
Wakes the eternal fount of human tears,
Sends us to watch some vision'd bed of death,
Hold the faint hand, and catch the parting breath,
Where those we prized the most, and loved the best,
Seem darkly sinking to the grave's long rest;
Lo! in our arms they fade, they faint, they die,
Before our eyes the funeral train sweeps by!
We hear the orphan's sob—the widow's wail—
O'er our dim senses woeful thoughts prevail,
Till, with a burst of grief, the spell we break,
And, weeping for th' imagined loss, awake.
Ah me! from dreams like these aroused at length,

How leaps the spirit to its former strength!
What memories crowd the newly conscious
brain,
What gleams of rapture, and what starts of pain!
Till from the soul the heavy mists stand clear,
All wanes and fades that seem'd so darkly drear
The sun's fair rays those shades of death destroy
And passionate thankfulness and tears of joy
Swell at our hearts, as, gazing on his beam,
We start, and cry aloud, "Thank Heaven,
'twas but a dream!"

But there are visions of a fairer kind,
Thoughts fondly cherish'd by the slumbering
mind,
Which, when they vanish from the waking
brain,
We close our eyes, and long to dream again.
Their dim voice calls to our forsaken side
Those who betray'd us, seeming true and tried·
Those whom the fast receding waves of time
Have floated from us; those who in the prime
And glory of our young life's eagle flight
Shone round like rays, encircling us with light,
And gave the bright similitude of truth
To fair illusions—vanish'd with our youth.
They bring again the tryst of early love,
(That passionate hope, all other hopes above!)
Bid the pale hair, long shrouded in the grave,
Round the young head in floating ringlets wave
And fill the air with echoes. Gentle words,
Low laughter, and the singing of sweet birds.

Come round us then; and dropping of light
boughs,
Whose shadow could not cool our burning brows,
And lilac-blossoms, scenting the warm air,
And long laburnums, fragile, bright, and fair;
And murmuring breezes through the green
leaves straying,
And rippling waters in the sunshine playing,
All that around our slumbering sense can fling
The glory of some half-forgotten spring!
They bring again the fond approving gaze
Of old true friends, who mingled love with
praise;
When Fame (that cold bright guiding-star be
low)
Took from affection's light a borrow'd glow—
And, strong in all the might of earnest thought,
Through the long studious night untired we
wrought,
That others might the morning hours beguile,
With the fond triumph of their wondering smile.
What though those dear approving smiles be
gone,
What though we strive neglected and alone,
What though no voice *now* mourns our hope's
alloy,
Nor in that hour of triumph gives us joy?
In *dreams* the days return when this was not,
When strong affection sooth'd our toilsome lot:
Cheer'd, loved, admonish'd, lauded, we aspire,
And the sick soul regains its former fire.

Beneath the influence of this fond spell,
Happy, contented, bless'd, we seem to dwell;
Sweet faces shine with love's own tender ray,
Which frown, or coldly turn from us, by day;
The lonely orphan hears a parent's voice;
Sad childless mothers once again rejoice;
The poor deserted seems a happy bride;
And the long parted wander side by side.

Ah, vain deceit; Awakening with a start,
Sick grows the beatings of the troubled heart;
Silence, like some dark mantle, drops around,
Quenching th' imagined voice's welcome sound,
Again the soul repeats its old farewells,
Again recalls sad hours and funeral knells;
Again, as daylight opens on their view,
The orphan shrinks, the mother mourns anew;
Till clear we feel, as fades the morning star,
How left, how lonely, how oppress'd we are!

And other dreams exist, more vague and bright
Than MEMORY ever brought to cheer the night;—
Most to the young and happy do they come,
To those who know no shelter but of home;
To those of whom the inspired writer spoke,
When from his lips the words prophetic broke,
Which (conscious of the strong and credulous spell
Experience only in the heart can quell)
Promised the nearer glimpse of perfect truth
Not to cold wisdom but to fervent youth

Each, in their measure, caught its fitful gleams—
The young saw visions, and the old dream'd dreams.

The young! Oh! what should wandering fancy bring
In life's first spring-time but the thoughts of spring?
World without winter, blooming amaranth bowers,
Garlands of brightness wreath'd from changeless flowers;
Where shapes like angels wander to and fro,
Unwing'd, but glorious, in the noontide glow,
Which steeps the hills, the dales, the earth, the sea,
In one soft flood of golden majesty.
In this world,—so create,—no sighs nor tears,—
No sadness brought with lapse of varying years,—
No cold betrayal of the trusting heart,—
No knitting up of love fore-doom'd to part,—
No pain, deformity, nor pale disease,—
No wars,—no tyranny,—nor fears that freeze
The rapid current of the restless blood,—
Nor effort scorn'd,—nor act misunderstood,—
No dark remorse for ever-haunting sin,—
But all at peace without,—at rest within;
And hopes which gild Thought's wildest waking hours,
Scatter'd around us carelessly as flowers.

Oh! Paradise, in vain didst thou depart·
Thine image still is stamp'd on every heart!

Though mourning man in vain may seek to trace
The site of that which *was* his dwelling-place,
Though the four glittering rivers *now* divide
No realms of beauty with their rolling tide.
Each several life yet opens with the view
Of that unblighted world where Adam drew
The breath of being: in each several mind,
However cramp'd, and fetter'd, and confined,
The innate power of beauty folded lies,
And, like a bud beneath the summer skies,
Blooms out in youth through many a radiant day
Though in life's winter frost it dies away.

From such a vision, bright with all the fame
Her youth, her innocence, her hope could frame,
The maiden woke: and, when her shadowy gaze
Had lost the dazzled look of wild amaze
Turn'd on her mother when she first awoke,
Thus to her questioning glance she answering spoke:—

"Methought, oh! gentle Mother, by thy side
I dwelt no more as now, but through a wide
And sweet world wander'd; nor even then alone;
For ever in that dream's soft light stood one,
I know not who,—yet most familiar seem'd
The fond companionship of which I dream'd;
A Brother's love, is but a name to me;
A Father's brighten'd not my infancy;
To me in childhood's years, no stranger's face
Took, from long habit, friendship's holy grace•

My life hath still been lone, and needed not,
Heaven knows, more perfect love than was my lot,
In thy dear heart: how dream'd I then, sweet Mother,
Of any love but thine, who knew no other?

"We seem'd, this shadow and myself, to be
Together by the blue and boundless sea;
No settled home was present to my thought—
No other form my clouded fancy brought;
This one Familiar Presence still beguiled
My every thought, and look'd on me and smiled,
Fair stretch'd in beauty lay the glittering strand,
With low green copses sloping from the land;
And tangled underwood and sunny fern,
And flowers whose humble names none cared to learn,
Small starry wild flowers, white and gold and blue,
With leaves turn'd crimson by the autumual hue,
Bask'd in the fervor of the noontide glow,
Wnose hot rays pierced the thirsty roots below.
The floating nautilus rose clear and pale,
As though a spirit trimm'd its fairy sail,
White and transparent; and beyond it gleam'd
Such light as never yet on Ocean beam'd:
And pink-lipp'd shells, and many color'd weeds,
And long brown bulbous things like jaspar beads,
And glistening pearls in beauty faint and fair,
And all things strange, and wonderful, and rare,
Whose true existence travellers make known,

Seem'd scatter'd there, and easily my own.
And then we wove our ciphers in the sands,
All fondly intertwined by loving hands;
And laugh'd to see the rustling snow-white spray
Creep o'er the names, and wash their trace away.
And the storm came not, though the white foam curl'd
In lines of brightness far along the coast;
Though many a ship, with swelling sails unfurl'd,
From the mid-sea to sheltering haven cross'd;
Though the wild billows heaved, and rose, and broke,
One o'er the other with a restless sound,
And the deep spirit of the wind awoke,
Ruffling in wrath each glassy verdant mound;
While onward roll'd that army of huge waves,
Until the foremost, with exulting roar,
Rose, proudly crested, o'er his brother slaves,
And dash'd triumphant on the groaning shore!
For then the Moon rose up, Night's mournful Queen,
'Walking with white feet o'er the troubled Sea,'
And all grew still again, as she had been
Heaven's messenger to bring Tranquility;
Till, pale and tender, on the glistening main
She sank and smiled like one who loves in vain.
And still we linger'd by that shadowy strand,
Happy, yet full of thought, hand link'd in hand;

The hush'd waves rippling softly at our feet,
The night-breeze freshening o'er the summer's
heat;
With our hearts beating, and our gazing eyes
Fix'd on the star-light of those deep blue skies,
Blessing 'the year, the hour, the place the
time;'
While sounded, faint and far, some turret's
midnight chime.

"It pass'd, that vision of the Ocean's might!
I know not how, for in my slumbering mind
There was no movement, all was shifting light,
Through which we floated with the wander-
ing wind;
And, still together, in a different scene,
We look'd on England's woodland, fresh and
green.

"No perfume of the cultured rose was there,
Wooing the senses with its garden smell,—
Nor snow-white lily,—called so proudly fair,
Though by the poor man's cot she loves to
dwell,
Nor finds his little garden scant of room
To bid her stately buds in beauty bloom;—
Nor jasmin, with her pale stars shining through
The myrtle darkness of her leaf's green hue,—
Nor helitrope, whose gray and heavy wreath
Mimics the orchard blossoms' fruity breath—
Nor clustering dahlia, with its scentless flower

Cheating the heart through autumn's faded
hours,—
Nor bright chrysanthimum, whose train'd array
Still makes the rich man's winter path look gay,
And bows its hardy head when wild winds blow,
To free its petals from the fallen snow;—
Nor yet carnation;"—

(Thou, beloved of all
The plants that thrive at Art or Nature's call,
By one who greets thee with a weary sigh
As the dear friend of happy days gone by;
By one who names thee last, but loves thee
first,
Of all the flowers a garden ever nursed;
The mute remembrancer and gentle token
Of links which heavy hands have roughly
broken,
Welcomed through many a Summer with the
same
Unalter'd gladness as when first ye came,
And welcomed still, though—as in later years
We often welcome pleasant things—with tears!)

I wander! In the Dream these had no place—
Nor Sorrow:—all was Nature's freshest grace.

"There, wild geranium, with its woolly stem
And aromatic breath, perfumed the glade;
And fairy speedwell, like some sapphire gem,
Lighted with purple sparks the hedge-row's
shade;
And woodbine, with her tinted calyxes,

And dog-rose glistening with the dews of
morn,
And tangled wreaths of tufted clematis,
Whose blossoms pale the careless eye may
scorn,
(As green and light her fairy mantles fall
To hide the rough hedge or the crumbling wall,)
But in whose breast the laden wild-bees dive
For the best riches of their teeming hive:
"There, sprang the sunny cricket; there,
was spread
The fragile silver of the spider's thread,
Stretching from blade to blade of emerald grass,
Unbroken, till some human footstep pass;
There, by the rippling stream that murmur'd on,
Now seen, now hidden—half in light, half Sun—
The darting dragon-fly, with sudden gleam,
Shot, as it went, a gold and purple beam;
And the fish leap'd within the deeper pool,
And the green trees stretch'd out their branches
cool,
Where many a bird hush'd in her peopled nest
The unfledged darlings of her feather'd breast,
Listening her mate's clear song, in that sweet
grove
Where all around breathed happiness and love!

"And while we talk'd the summer hours flew
fast,
As hours may fly, with those whose love is
young;
Who fear no future, and who know no past

Dating existence from the hope that sprung
Up in their hearts with such a sudden light,
That all beyond shows dark and blank as night.
"Until methought we trod a wide flat heath,
Where yew and cypress darkly seem'd to wave
O'er countless tombs, so beautiful, that death
Seem'd here to make a garden of the grave!
All that is holy, tender, full of grace,
Was sculptured on the monuments around,
And many a line the musing eye could trace,
Which spoke unto the heart without a sound.
There lay the warrior and the son of song,
And there—in silence till the judgment-day—
The orator, whose all-persuading tongue
Had moved the nations with resistless sway
There slept pale men whom science taught to climb
Restlessly upward all their laboring youth;
Who left, half conquer'd, secrets which in time
Burst on mankind in ripe and glorious truth.
He that had gazed upon the steadfast stars,
And could foretell the dark eclipse's birth,
And when red comets in their blazing cars
Should sweep above the awed and troubled earth:—
He that had sped brave vessels o'er the seas,
Which swiftly bring the wanderer to his home,
Uncanvass'd ships, which move without a breeze,
Their bright wheels dashing through the ocean foam:—

All, who in this life's bounded brief career
  Had shone amongst or served their fellow-men,
And left a name embalm'd in glory here,
  Lay calmly buried on that magic plain.
And he who wander'd with me in my dream,
  Told me their histories as we onward went,
Till the grave shone with such a hallow'd beam,
  Such pleasure with their memory seem'd blent,
That, when we look'd to heaven, our upward eyes
With no funeral sadness mock'd the skies!

"Then, change of scene, and time, and place once more;
  And by a Gothic window, richly bright,
Whose stain'd armorial bearings on the floor
  Flung the quaint tracery of their color'd light,
We sate together: his most noble head
  Bent o'er the storied tome of other days,
And still he commented on all we read,
  And taught me what to love, and what to praise,
Then Spenser made the summer-day seem brief,
  Or Milton sounded with a loftier song,
Then Cowper charm'd, with lays of gentle grief,
  Or rough old Dryden roll'd the hour along.
Or, in his varied beauty dearer still,
Sweet Shakspeare changed the world around at will;
And we forgot the sunshine of that room

To sit with Jacquez in the forest gloom;
To look abroad with Juliet's anxious eye
For her boy-lover 'neath the moonlight sky;
Stand with Macbeth upon the haunted heath
Or weep for gentle Desdemona's death;
Watch, on bright Cydnus' wave, the glittering sheen
And silken sails of Egypt's wanton queen;
Or roam with Ariel through that island strange
Where spirits, and not men, were wont to range,
Still struggling on through brake, and bush, and hollow,
Hearing that sweet voice calling—'Follow! follow!'

"Nor were there wanting lays of other lands,
For these were all familiar in his hands:
And Dante's dream of horror work'd its spell,—
And Petrarch's sadness on our bosom fell,—
And prison'd Tasso's—he, the coldly-loved,
The madly-loving! he, so deeply proved
By many a year of darkness, like the grave,
For her who dared not plead, or would not save,
For her who thought the poet's suit brought shame,
Whose passion hath immortalized her name!
And Egmont, with his noble heart betray'd,—
And Carlos, haunted by a murder'd shade,—
And Faust's strange legend, sweet and wond'rous wild,
Stole many a tear:—Creation's loveliest child'
Guileless, ensnared, and tempted Margaret,

Who could peruse thy fate with eyes unwet?
"Then, through the lands we read of, far away,
The vision led me all a summer's day:
And we look'd round on southern Italy,
Where her dark head the graceful cypress rears
In arrowy straightness and soft majesty,
And the sun's face a mellower glory wears;
Bringing, where'er his warm light richly shines,
Sweet odors from the gum-distilling pines;
And casting o'er white palaces a glow,
Like morning's hue on mountain-peaks of snow.

"Those palaces! how fair their columns rose!
Their courts, cool fountains, and wide porticos!
And ballustraded roofs, whose very form
Told what an unknown stranger was the storm!
In one of these we dwelt: its painted walls
A master's hand had been employed to trace;
Its long cool range of shadowy marble halls
Was fill'd with statues of most living grace;
While on its ceiling roll'd the fiery car
Of the bright day-god, chasing night afar,—
Or Jove's young favorite, toward Olympus' height
Soar'd with the Eagle's dark majestic flight,—
Or fair Apollo's harp seem'd freshly strung,
All heaven group'd round him, listening while he sung.

"So, in the garden's plann'd and planted bound
All wore the aspect of enchanted ground ;
Thick orange-groves, close arching over head,
Shelter'd the paths our footsteps loved to tread ;
Or ilex-trees shut out, with shadow sweet,
Th' oppressive splendor of the noontide heat.
Through the bright vista, at each varying turn,
Gleam'd the white statue, or the graceful urn ;
And, paved with many a curved and twisted line
Of fair Mosaic's strange and quaint design,
Terrace on terrace rose, with steep so slight,
That scarce the pausing eye inquired the height,
Till stretch'd beneath in far perspective lay
The glittering city and the deep blue bay !
Then as we turn'd again to groves and bowers,
(Rich with the perfume of a thousand flowers,)
The sultry day was cheated of its force
By the sweet winding of some streamlet's course :
From sculptured arch, and ornamented walls,
Rippled a thousand tiny waterfalls,
While here and there an open basin gave
Rest to the eye and freshness to the wave ;
Here, high above the imprison'd waters, stood
Some imaged Naiad, guardian of the flood ;
There, in a cool and grotto-like repose,
The sea-born goddess from her shell arose ;
Or river-god his fertile urn display'd,
Gushing at distance through the long arcade,—
Or Triton, lifting his wild conch on high,
Spouted his silver tribute to the sky,

Or, lovelier still, (because to Nature true,
Even in the thought creative genius drew,)
Some statue-nymph, her bath of beauty o'er,
Stood gently bending by the rocky shore,
And, like Bologna's sweet and graceful dream,
From her moist hair wrung out the living stream.

" Bright was the spot! and still we linger'd on
Unwearied, till the summer-day was done;
Till He, who, when the morning dew was wet,
In glory rose—in equal glory set.
Fair sank his light, unclouded to the last,
And o'er that land its glow of beauty cast;
And the sweet breath of evening air went forth
To cool the bosom of the fainting earth;
To bid the pale-leaved olives lightly wave
Upon their seaward slope (whose waters lave
With listless gentleness the golden strand,
And scarcely leave, and scarce return to land;)
Or with its wings of freshness, wandering round,
Visit the heights of many a villa crown'd,
Where the still pine and cypress, side by side.
Look from their distant hills on Ocean's tide.

"The cypress and the pine! Ah, still I see
These thy green children, lovely Italy!
Nature's dear favorites, allow'd to wear
Their summer hue throughout the circling year
And oft, when wandering out at even-time
To watch the sunsets of a colder clime,
As the dim landscape fades and grows more faint

Fancy's sweet power a different scene shall
paint;
Enrich with deeper tints the colors given
To the pale beauty of our English heaven,—
Bid purple mountains rise among the clouds,
Or deem their mass some marble palace
shrouds,—
Trace on the red horizon's level line,
In outlines dark, the high majestic pine,—
And hear, amid the groups of English trees,
His sister cypress murmuring to the breeze!

"Never again shall evening, sweet and still,
Gleam upon river, mountain, rock, or hill,—
Never again shall fresh and budding spring,
Or brighter summer, hue of beauty bring,
In this, the clime where 'tis my lot to dwell,
But shall recall, as by a magic spell,
Thy scenes, dear land of poetry and song!
Bid thy fair statues on my memory throng;
Thy glorious pictures gleam upon my sight
Like fleeting shadows o'er the summer light
And send my haunted heart to dwell once more,
Clad and entranced by thy delightful shore—
Thy shore, where rolls that blue and tideless sea,
Bright as thyself, thou radiant Italy!

"And there (where Beauty's spirit sure had
birth,
Though she hath wander'd since upon the
earth,
And scatter'd, as she pass'd, some sparks of
thought,

Such as of old her sons of genius wrought,
To show what strength the immortal soul can
wield
E'en here, in this its dark and narrow field,
And fills us with a fond inquiring thirst
To see that land which claim'd her triumphs
first)
Music was brought—with soft impressive
power—
To fill with varying joy the varying hour.
We welcomed it; for welcome still to all
It comes, in cottage, court, or lordly hall;
And in the long bright summer evenings, oft
We sate and listened to some measure soft
From many instruments; or, faint and lone,
(Touch'd by his gentle hand, or by my own,)
The little lute its chorded notes would send
Tender and clear; and with our voices blend
Cadence so true, that, when the breeze swept by,
One mingled echo floated on its sigh!

"And still as day by day we saw depart,
I was the living idol of his heart:
How to make joy a portion of the air
That breathed around me, seem'd his only care.
For me the harp was strung, the page was turn'd;
For me the morning rose, the sunset burn'd;
For me the Spring put out her verdant suit;
For me the Summer flower, the Autumn fruit,
The very world seem'd mine, so mighty strove
For my contentment, that enduring love.

"I see him still, dear mother! Still I hear
That voice so deeply soft, so strangely clear;
Still in the air wild wandering echoes float,
And bring my dream's sweet music note for note!
Oh! shall those sounds no more my fancy bless,
Which fill my heart and on my memory press?
Shall I no more those sunset clouds behold,
Floating like bright transparent thrones of gold?
The skies, the seas, the hills of glorious blue;
The glades and groves, with glories shining through;
The bands of red and purple, richly seen
Athwart the sky of pale, faint, gem-like green;
When the breeze slept, the earth lay hush'd and still,
When the low sun sank slanting from the hill,
And slow and amber-tinged the moon uprose,
To watch his farewell hour in glory close?
Is all that radiance past—gone by forever—
And must there in its stead forever be
The gray, sad sky, the cold and clouded river,
And dismal dwellings by the wintry sea?
E'er half a summer, altering day by day,
In fickle brightness, here, hath pass'd away!
And was that form (whose love might still sustain)
Naught but a vapor of the dreaming brain?
Would I had slept for ever!"
Sad she sigh'd;
To whom the mournful mother thus replied:—

"Upbraid not Heaven, whose wisdom thus would rule

A world whose changes are the soul's best
school:
All dream like thee, and 'tis for Mercy's sake
That those who dream the wildest, soonest
wake;
All deem Perfection's system would be found
In giving earthly sense no stint or bound;
All look for happiness beneath the sun,
And each expects what God hath given to *none*.

"In what an idle luxury of joy
Would thy spoil'd heart its useless hours employ!
In what a selfish loneliness of light
Wouldst thou exist, read we thy dream aright!
How hath thy sleeping spirit broke the chain
Which knits thy human lot to other's pain,
And made this world of peopled millions seem
For thee and for the lover of thy dream!

"Think not my heart with cold indifference
heard
The various feelings which in thine have stirr'd,
Or that its sad and weary currents know
Faint sympathy, except for human woe:
Well have the dormant echoes of my breast
Answer'd the joys thy gentle voice express'd;
Conjured a vision of the stately mate
With whom the flattering vision link'd thy fate;
And follow'd thee through grove and woodland
wild,

Where so much natural beauty round thee
smiled.

" What man so worldly-wise, or chill'd by age,
Who, bending o'er the faint descriptive page,
Recalls not such a scene in some far nook—
(Whereon his eyes, perchance, no more shall
look ;)
Some hawthorn copse, some gnarl'd majestic
tree,
The favorite play-place of his infancy ?
Who has not felt for Cowper's sweet lament,
When twelve years' course their cruel change
had sent ;
When his fell'd poplars gave no further shade,
And low on earth the blackbird's nest was laid ;
When in a desert sunshine, bare and blank,
Lay the green field and river's mossy bank ;
And melody of bird or branch no more
Rose with the breeze that swept along the shore ?

" Few are the hearts, (nor theirs of kindliest
frame,)
On whom fair Nature holds not such a claim ;
And oft, in after-life, some simple thing—
A bank of primroses in early spring—
The tender scent which hidden violets yield—
The sight of cowslips in a meadow-field—
Or young laburnum's pendant yellow chain—
May bring the favorite play-place back again

Our youthful mates are gone; some dead, some
changed,
With whom that pleasant spot was gladly ranged;
Ourselves, perhaps, more alter'd e'en than
they—
But *there* still blooms the blossom-showering
May;
There still along the hedge-row's verdant line
The linnet sings, the thorny brambles twine;
Still in the copse a troop of merry elves
Shout—the gay image of our former selves;
And still, with sparkling eyes and eager hands
Some rosy urchin high on tiptoe stands,
And plucks the ripest berries from the bough—
Which tempts a different generation now!

"What though no *real* beauty haunt that spot
By graver minds beheld and noticed not?
Can we forget that once to our young eyes
It wore the aspect of a Paradise?
No; still around its hallow'd precinct lives
The fond mysterious charm that memory gives;
The man recalls the feelings of the boy,
And clothes the meanest flower with freshness
and with joy.

"Nor think by elder hearts forgotten quite
Love's whisper'd words; youth's sweet and
strange delight;
They live—though after-memories fade away;
They live to cheer life's slow declining day;

Haunting the widow by her lonely hearth,
As, meekly smiling at her children's mirth,
She spreads her fair thin hands toward the fire,
To seek the warmth their slacken'd veins require:
Or gladdening her to whom Heaven's mercy spares
Her old companion with his silver hairs;
And while he dozes—changed, and dull, and weak—
And his hush'd grandchild signs, but dares not speak.—
Bidding her watch, with many a tender smile,
The wither'd form which slumbers all the while

"Yes! sweet the voice of those we loved! the tone
Which cheers our memory as we sit alone,
And will not leave us; the o'er-mastering force,
Whose under-current's strange and hidden course
Bids some chance word, by colder hearts forgot,
Return—and still return—yet weary not
The ear which wooes its sameness! How, when Death
Hath stopp.d with ruthless hands some precious breath,
The memory of the voice he hath destroy'd
Lives in our souls, as in an aching void!
How, through the varying fate of after-years,
When stifled sorrow weeps but casual tears,
If some stray tone seem *like* the voice we know

The heart leaps up with answer faint and true!
Greeting again that sweet, long-vanish'd sound,
As, in earth's nooks of ever-haunted ground,
Strange accident, or man's capricious will,
Wakes the lone echoes, and they answer still!

"Oh! what a shallow fable cheats the age,
When the lost lover, on the motley stage,
Wrapp'd from his mistress in some quaint disguise,
Deceives her ears, because he cheats her eyes!
Rather, if all could fade which charm'd us first,—
If, by some magic stroke, some plague-spot cursed,
All outward semblance left the form beloved
A wreck unrecognised, and half disproved,
At the dear sound of that familiar voice
Her waken'd heart should tremble and rejoice,
Leap to its faith at once,—and spurn the doubt
Which, on such showing, barr'd his welcome out!

"And if even *words* are sweet, what, what is song,
When lips we love, the melody prolong?
How thrills the soul, and vibrates to that lay,
Swells with the glorious sound, or dies away!
How, to the cadence of the simplest words
That ever hung upon the wild harp's chords,
The breathless heart lies listening; as it felt
All life within it on that music dwelt

And hush'd the beating pulse's rapid power
By its own will, for that enchanted hour!

"Ay! *then* to those who love the science well,
Music becomes a passion and a spell!
Music, the tender child of rudest times,
The gentle native of all lands and climes;
Who hymns alike man's cradle and his grave,
Lulls the low cot, or peals along the nave;
Cheers the poor peasant, who his native hills
With wild Tyrolean echoes sweetly fills;
Inspires the Indian's low monotonous chant,
Weaves skilful melodies, for Luxury's haunt;
And still, through all these changes, lives the same,
Spirit without a home, without a name,
Coming, where all is discord, strife, and sin,
To prove some innate harmony within
Our listening souls; and lull the heaving breast
With the dim vision of an unknown rest!

"But, dearest child, though many a joy be given
By the pure bounty of all-pitying Heaven,—
Though sweet emotions in our hearts have birth,
As flowers are spangled on the lap of earth,—
Though, with the flag of Hope and Triumph hung
High o'er our heads, we start when life is young,
And onward cheer'd, by sense, and sight, and sound,

Like a launch'd bark, we enter with a bound,
Yet must the dark cloud lour, the tempest fall,
And the same chance of shipwreck waits for all.
Happy are they who leave the harboring land
Not for a summer voyage, hand in hand,
Pleasure's light slaves: but with an earnest eye
Exploring all the future of their sky;
That so, when Life's career at length is past,
To the right haven they may steer at last,
And safe from hidden rock, or open gale,
Lay by the oar, and furl the slacken'd sail,—
To anchor deeply on that tranquil shore
Where vexing storms can never reach them more!

"Wouldst thou be singled out by partial Heaven
The ONE to whom a cloudless lot is given?
Look round the world, and see what fate is there,
Which justice can pronounce exempt from care:
Though bright they bloom to empty outward show
There lurks in each some canker-worm of woe;
Still by some thorn the onward step is cross'd,
Nor least repining those who 're envied most:
The poor have struggling, toil, and wounded pride,
Which seeks, and seeks in vain, its rags to hide;
The rich, cold jealousies, intrigues, and strife,
And heart-sick discontent which poisons life;
The loved are parted by the hand of Death,
The hated live to curse each other's breath:
The wealthy noble mourns the want of heirs;

While, each the object of incessant prayers,
Gay, hardy sons, around the widow's board,
With careless smiles devour her scanty hoard;
And hear no sorrow in her stifled sigh,
And see no terror in her anxious eye,—
While *she* in fancy antedates the time
When, scatter'd far and wide in many a clime,
These heirs to nothing but their Father's name
Must earn their bread, and struggle hard for fame;
To sultry India sends her fair-hair'd boy—
Sees the dead desk another's youth employ—
And parts with one to sail the uncertain main,
Never perhaps on earth to meet again!

"Nor e'en does Love, whose fresh and radiant beam
Gave added brightness to thy wandering dream,
Preserve from bitter touch of ills unknown,
But rather brings strange sorrows of its own.
Various the ways in which our souls are tried;
Love often fails where most our faith relied;
Some wayward heart may win, without a thought,
That which thine own by sacrifice hath bought;
May carelessly aside the treasure cast,
And yet be madly worshipp'd to the last;
Whilst thou, forsaken, grieving, left to pine,
Vainly may'st claim his plighted faith as thine:
Vainly his idol's charms with thine compare,
And know thyself as young, as bright, as fair·
Vainly in jealous pangs consume thy day,

And waste the sleepless night in tears away
Vainly with forced indulgence strive to smile
In the cold world, heart-broken all the while,
Or from its glittering and unquiet crowd,
Thy brain on fire, thy spirit crush'd and bow'd,
Creep home unnoticed, there to weep alone,
Mock'd by a claim which gives thee not thine own,
Which leaves thee bound through all thy blighted youth
To him whose perjured soul hath broke its truth;
While the just world, beholding thee bereft,
Scorns—not his sin—but *thee*, for being left!

"Ah! never to the Sensualist appeal,
Nor deem his frozen bosom aught can feel.
Affection, root of all fond memories,
Which bids what once hath charm'd for ever please,
He knows not: all thy beauty could inspire
Was but a sentiment of low desire:
If from thy cheek the rose's hue be gone,
How should love stay which loved for that alone?
Or, if thy youthful face be still as bright
As when it first entranced his eager sight,
Thou art *the same;* there is thy fault, thy crime,
Which fades the charms yet spared by rapid Time,
Talk to him of the happy days gone by,
Conceal'd aversion chills his shrinking eye;
While in thine agony thou still dost rave,
Impatient wishes doom thee to the grave;

And if his cold and selfish thought had power
T' accelerate the fatal final hour,
The silent murder were already done,
And thy white tomb would glitter in the sun.
What wouldst thou hold by? What is it to him
That for his sake thy weeping eyes are dim?
His pall'd and weary senses rove apart,
And for his heart—thou never *hadst* his heart.

"True, there is better love, whose balance just
Mingles Soul's instinct with our grosser dust,
And leaves affection, strengthening day by day,
Firm to assault, impervious to decay.
To such, a star of hope thy love shall be
Whose steadfast light he still desires to see;
And age shall vainly mar thy beauty's grace,
Or wantons plot to steal into thy place,
Or wild Temptation, from her hidden bowers,
Fling o'er his path her bright but poisonous flowers,—
Dearer to him than all who thus beguile,
Thy faded face, and thy familiar smile;
Thy glance, which still hath welcomed him for years,
Now bright with gladness, and now dim with tears!
And if (for we are weak) division come
On wings of discord to that happy home,
Soon is the painful hour of anger past,
Too sharp, too strange an agony to last;
And, like some river's bright abundant tide

Which art or accident hath forced aside,
The well-springs of affection, gushing o'er,
Back to their natural channels flow once more.

"Ah! sad it is when one thus link'd departs!
When Death, that mighty severer of true hearts,
Sweeps through the halls so lately loud in mirth,
And leaves pale Sorrow weeping by the hearth!
Bitter it is to wander there alone,
To fill the vacant place, the empty chair,
With a dear vision of the loved one gone,
And start to see it vaguely melt in air!
Bitter to find all joy that once hath been
Double its value when 'tis pass'd away,—
To feel the blow which Time should make less keen
Increase its burden each successive day,—
To need good counsel, and to miss the voice,
The ever trusted, and the ever true,
Whose tones were wont to cheer our faltering choice,
And show what holy Virtue bade us do,—
To bear deep wrong and bow the widow'd head
In helpless anguish, no one to defend;
Or worse,—in lieu of him, the kindly dead,
Claim faint assistance from some lukewarm friend—
Yet scarce perceive the extent of all our loss
Till the fresh tomb be green with gathering moss—
Till many a morn have met our sadden'd eyes,
With none to say "Good morrow;"—many an eve

Send its red glory through the tranquil skies,
Each bringing with it deeper cause to grieve!

"This is a destiny which may be thine—
The common grief: God will'd it should be mine:
Short was the course our happy love had run,
And hard it was to say 'Thy will be done!'

"Yet those whom man, not God, hath parted, know
A heavier pang, a more enduring woe;
No softening memory mingles with *their* tears,
Still the wound rankles on through dreary years,
Still the heart feels, in bitterest hours of blame,
It dares not curse the long-familiar name;
Still, vainly free, through many a cheerless day,
From weaker ties turn helplessly away,
Sick for the smiles that bless'd its home of yore,
The natural joys of life that come no more;
And, all bewilder'd by the abyss, whose gloom
Dark and impassable as is the tomb,
Lies stretch'd between the future and the past,—
Sinks into deep and cold despair at last.

"Heaven give thee poverty, disease, or death,
Each varied ill that waits on human breath,
Rather than bid thee linger out thy life
In the long toil of such unnatural strife.
To wander through the world unreconciled,

Heart weary as a spirit-broken child,
And think it were an hour of bliss like neaven
If thou could'st *die*—forgiving and forgiven,—
Or with a feverish hope of anguish born,
(Nerving thy mind to feel indignant scorn
Of all the cruel foes who 'twixt ye stand,
Holding thy heartstrings with a reckless hand,)
Steal to his presence, now unseen so long,
And claim *his* mercy who hath dealt the wrong!
Into the aching depths of thy poor heart
Dive, as it were, even to the roots of pain,
And wrench up thoughts that tear thy soul apart,
And burn like fire through thy bewilder'd brain.
Clothe them in passionate words of wild appeal
To teach thy fellow-creature *how* to feel,—
Pray, weep, exhaust thyself in maddening tears,—
Recall the hopes, the influences of years,—
Kneel, dash thyself upon the senseless ground.
Writhe as the worm writhes with dividing wound,—
Invoke the heaven that knows thy sorrow's truth,
By all the softening memories of youth—
By every hope that cheer'd thine earlier day—
By every tear that washes wrath away—
By every old remembrance long gone by—
By every pang that makes thee yearn to die;
And learn at length how deep and stern a blow
Near hands can strike, and yet no pity show!

"Oh! weak to suffer, savage to inflict,
Is man's commingling nature; hear him now

Some transient trial of his life depict,
Hear him in holy rites a suppliant bow ;
See him shrink back from sickness and from pain,
And in his sorrow to his God complain ;
'Remit my trespass, spare my sin,' he cries,
'All-merciful, Almighty, and All-wise ;
Quench this affliction's bitter whelming tide,
Draw out thy barbed arrow from my side :'—
—And rises from that mockery of prayer
To hale some brother-debtor to despair!

"May this be spared thee ! Yet be sure, my child,
(Howe'er that dream thy fancy hath beguiled,)
Some sorrow lurks to cloud thy future fate ;
Thy share of tears,—come early or come late,—
Must still be shed ; and 'twere as vain a thing
To ask of Nature one perpetual spring
As to evade those sad autumnal hours,
Or deem thy path of life should bloom, all flowers."

She ceased: and that fair maiden heard the truth
With the fond passionate despair of youth,
Which, new to suffering, gives its sorrow vent
In outward signs and bursts of wild lament :—

"If this be so, then, mother, let me die
Ere yet the glow hath faded from my sky !
Let me die young ; before the holy trust

In human kindness crumbles into dust;
Before I suffer what I have not earn'd,
Or see by treachery my truth return'd;
Before the love I live for, fades away;
Before the hopes I cherish'd most, decay;
Before the withering touch of fearful change
Makes some familiar face look cold and strange,
Or some dear heart, close knitted to my own,
By perishing, hath left me more alone!
Though death be bitter, I can brave its pain
Better than all which threats if I remain:
While my soul, freed from ev'ry chance of ill,
Soars to that God whose high mysterious will
Sent me, foredoom'd to grief, with wandering feet,
To group my way through all this fair deceit!"

Her parent heard the words with grieved amaze,
And thus return'd, with calm reproving gaze:—

"Blaspheme not Heaven with rash impatient speech,
Nor deem, at thine own hour, its rest to reach,
Unhappy child! The full appointed time
Is His to choose; and when the sullen chime,
And deep-toned striking of the funeral bell,
Thy fate to earthly ears shall sadly tell,
Oh! may the death thou talk'st of as a boon,
Find thee prepared,—nor come even then too soon!

"True, ere thou meet'st that long and dreamless sleep,
Thy heart must ache—thy weary eyes must weep:
It is our human lot! The fariest child
That e'er on loving mother brightly smiled,—
Most watch'd, most tended—ere his eyelids close,
Hath had his little share of infant woes,
And dies familiar with the sense of grief,
Though for all else his life hath been too brief!
But shall we therefore, murmuring against God,
Question the justice of his chastening rod,
And look to earthly joys as though *they* were
The prize immortal souls were given to share?
"Oh! were such joys and this vain world alone
The term of human hope—where, where would be
The victims of some tyranny unknown,
Who sank, still conscious that the *mind* was free?
They that have lain in dungeons years on years,
No voice to cheer their darkness,—they whose pain
Of horrid torture wrung forth blood with tears,
Murder'd, perhaps, for some rapacious gain,—
They who have stood, bound to the martyr's stake,
While the sharp flames ate through the blistering skin,—
They that have bled for some high cause's sake,—

They that have perish'd for another's sin,
And from the scaffold to that God appeal'd
To whom the naked heart is all reveal'd,
Against the shortening of life's narrow span
By the blind rage and false decree of man?
And where obscurer sufferers—they who slept
And left no name on history's random page,
But in God's book of reckoning, sternly kept,
Live on from year to year, from age to age?
The poor—the laboring poor! whose weary lives,
Through many a freezing night and hungry day,
Are a reproach to him who only strives
In luxury to waste his hours away,—
The patient poor! whose insufficient means
Make sickness dreadful, yet by whose low bed
Oft in meek prayers some fellow sufferer leans,
And trusts in Heaven while destitute of bread;
The workhouse orphan, left without a friend;
Or weak forsaken child of want and sin,
Whose helpless life begins, as it must end,
By men disputing who shall take it in;
Who clothe, who aid that spark to linger here,
Which for mysterious purpose God hath given
To struggle through a day of toil and fear,
And meet him—with the proudest--up in heaven!
These were, and are not:—shall we therefore deem
That they have vanish'd like a sleeper's dream?

Or that one half creation is to know
Luxurious joy, and others only woe,
And so go down into the common tomb,
With none to question their unequal doom?
Shall we give credit to a thought so fond?
Ah! no—the world beyond—the world beyond!
There, shall the desolate heart regain its own!
There, the oppress'd shall stand before God's throne!
There, when the tangled web is all explain'd,
Wrong suffer'd, pain inflicted, grief disdain'd,
Man's proud mistaken judgments and false scorn
Shall melt like mists before uprising morn,
And holy truth stand forth serenely bright,
In the rich flood of God's eternal light!

"Then shall the Lazarus of the earth have rest—
The rich man judgment—and the grieving breast
Deep peace for ever. Therefore look thou not
So much to what on earth shall be thy lot,
As to thy fate hereafter,—to that day
When like a scroll this world shall pass away,
And what thou here hast done, or here enjoy'd,
Import but to thy *soul*:—all else destroy'd!

"And have thou faith in human nature still;
Though evil thoughts abound, and acts of ill;
Though innocence in sorrow shrouded be,
And tyranny's strong step walk bold and free!
For many a kindly generous deed is done

Which leaves no record underneath the sun—
Self-abnegating love and humble worth,
Which yet shall consecrate our sinful earth!
He that deals blame, and yet forgets to praise,
Who sets brief storms against long summer-days,
Hath a sick judgment. Shall the usual joy
Be all forgot, and nought our minds employ,
Through the long course of ever-varing years,
But temporary pain and casual tears?
And shall we *all* condemn, and *all* distrust,
Because some men are false and some unjust?
Forbid it heaven! far better 'twere to be
Dupe of the fond impossibility
Of light and radiance which thy vision gave,
Than thus to live Suspicion's bitter slave.
Give credit to thy mortal brother's heart
For all the good than in thine own hath part,
And, cheerfully as honest prudence may,
Trust to his proffer'd hand's protecting stay:
For God, who made this teeming earth so full,
And made the proud dependent on the dull—
The strong upon the weak—thereby would show
One common bond should link us all below.

"And visit not with a severer scorn
Faults, whose deep root was with our nature born,
From which—though others woo'd thee just as vain—
Thou, differently tempted, didst abstain:
Nor dwell on points of creed—assuming right
To judge how holy in his Maker's sight

Is he who at a different altar bends ;
For hence have ris'n the bitterest feuds of friends,
The wildest wars of nations ; age on age
Hath desecrated thus dark History's page ;
And still (though not, perhaps, with fire and sword)
Reckless we raise 'The banner of the Lord !'
Mock Heaven's calm mercy by the plea we make,
That all is done for gentle Jesus' sake,—
Disturb the consciences of weaker men,—
Employ the scholar's art, the bigot's pen,—
And rouse the wrathful and the spirit-proud
To language bitter, vehement, and loud,
Whose unconvincing fury wounds the ear,
And seeking, with some sharp and haughty sneer,
How best the opposing party may be stung,—
Pleads for religion with a devil's tongue !

"Oh! shall God tolerate the meanest prayer
That humbly seeks his high supernal throne,
And man—presumptuous Pharisee—declare
His fellow's voice less welcome than his own ?
Is it a theme for wild and warring words
How best to satisfy the Maker's claim ?
In rendering to the Lord what is the Lord's,
Doth not the thought of violence bring shame ?
Think ye he gave the branching forest tree
To furnish fagots for the funeral pyre ?
Or bid his sunrise light the world, to see

Pale tortured victims perish there by fire?
No! oft on earth, dragg'd forth in pain to die,
The heretic may groan—the martyr bleed—
But, set before his Sovereign Judge on high,
'Tis man's *offence* condemns him, not his creed.
His first commandment was to worship Him;
His next—to love the creature He hath made:
How blind the eyes of those who read, how dim,
Who see not here religious fury stay'd!
From the proud *half*-fulfilment of his law
Sternly he turns away his awful face,
Nor will contentment from their service draw,
Who fail to grant a fellow-creature grace.
Haply the days of martyrdom are past,
But still we see, without a visible end,
The bitter warfare of opinion last,
Tho' God hath will'd that man should be man's friend.
Therefore do thou, e'er yet thy youthful heart
Be tinged with their revilings, safe retreat,
And in those fierce discussions bear no part,—
Odius in all—in woman most unmeet,—
But in the still dark night, and rising day,
Humbly collect thy thoughts, and humbly pray.

"And be not thou cast down, because thy lot
The glory of thy dream resembleth not.
Not for herself was woman first create,
Nor yet to be man's idol, but his mate.
Still from his birth his cradled bed she tends,
The first, the last, the faithfulest of friends;

Still finds her place in sickness or in woe,
Humble to comfort, strong to undergo;
Still in the depth of weeping sorrow tries
To watch his death-bed with her patient eyes!
And doubt not thou,—(although at times deceived,
Outraged, insulted, slander'd, crush'd, and grieved;
Too often made a victim or a toy,
With years of sorrow for an hour of joy;
Too oft forgot midst Pleasure's circling wiles,
Or only valued for her rosy smiles,—)
That in the frank and generous heart of man,
The place she holds accords with Heaven's high plan;
Still, if from wandering sin reclaim'd at all,
He sees in *her* the angel of recall;
Still, in the sad and serious hours of life,
Turns to the sister, mother, friend or wife;
Views with a heart of fond and trustful pride
His faithful partner by his calm fireside;
And oft, when barr'd of Fortune's fickle grace,
Blank ruin stares him darkly in the face,
Leans his faint head upon her kindly breast,
And owns her power to soothe him into rest,—
Owns what the gift of woman's love is worth
To cheer his toils and trials upon earth!

"Sure it is much, this delegated power
To be consoler of man's heaviest hour!
The guardian angel of a life of care,
Allow'd to stand 'twixt him and his despair!

Such service may be made a holy task;
And more, 'twere vain to hope, and rash to ask,
Therefore, oh! loved and lovely, be content,
And take thy lot, with joy and sorrow blent.
Judge none; yet let thy share of conduct be,
As knowing judgment shall be pass'd on thee
Here and hereafter; so, still undismay'd,
And guarded by thy sweet thoughts' tranquil shade,
Undazzled by the changeful rays which threw
Their light across thy path while life was new,
Thou shalt move sober on,—expecting less,
Therefore the more enjoying, happiness."

There was a pause; then, with a tremulous smile,
The maiden turn'd and press'd her mother's hand:—
"Shall I not bear what thou hast borne e'rewhile?
Shall I, rebellious, Heaven's high will withstand?
No! cheerly on, my wandering path I'll take,
Nor fear the destiny I did not make:
Though earthly joy grow dim—though pleasure waneth—
This thou hast taught thy child, that GOD remaineth!"

And from her mother's fond protecting side
She went into the world a youthful bride.

A DESTINY.

THERE was a lady, who had early wed
One whom she saw and loved in her bright youth,
When life was yet untried—and when he said
He, too, lov'd her, he spoke no more than truth;
He lov'd as well as baser nature can,—
But a mean heart and soul were in that man.

And they dwelt happily, if happy be
Not with harsh words to breed unnatural strife:
The cold world's Argus-watching failed to see
The flaw that dimm'd the lustre of their life;
Save that he seem'd tyrannical, tho' gay,
Restless and selfish in his love of sway.

The calm of conscious power was not in him;
But rather struggling into broader light,
The secret sense, they feel, however dim,
Whose chance position gives a sort of right
(As from the height of a prescriptive throne,)
To govern natures nobler than their own.

And as her youth waned slowly on, there fell
A nameless shadow on that lady's heart;
And those she lov'd the best (and she lov'd well,)
Had of her confidence nor share, nor part;
Her thoughts lay folded from life's lessening light,
Like the sweet flowers that close themselves at night

And men began to whisper evil things
Against the honor of her wedded mate;
That which had pass'd for youth's wild wanderings,
Showed more suspicious in his settled state;
Until at length,—he stood, at some chance game,
Discover'd,—branded with a Cheater's name.

Out, and away he slunk, with felon air;
Then, calling to him one who was his friend,
Bid him to that unblemish'd wife repair
And tell her what had chanced, and what the end;
How they must leave the country of their birth,
And hide,—in some more distant spot of earth.

It was a coward's thought: he could not bear
Himself to be narrator of his shame;
He that had trampled oft, now felt in fear
Of her who still must keep his blighted name,—
And shrank in fancy from that steadfast eye.
The window to a soul so pure and high.

She heard it. O'er her brow there pass'd a flush
Of sunset red; and then so white a hue,
So deadly pale, it seem'd as if no blush
Through that transparent cheek should shine anew;
As if the blood had frozen in that hour,
And her check'd pulse for ever lost its power.

And twice and once did she essay to speak;
And with a gesture almost of command,
(Though in its motion it was deadly weak)
She faintly lifted up her graceful hand:—
But then her soul came back to her, strength woke,
And with a low but even voice, she spoke:

"Go! say to him who dreamed of other chance,
That HERE none sit in judgment on his sin;
That to his door the world's scorn may advance,
And cloud his path, but doth not enter in.
Here dwell his Own: to share, to soothe disgrace;"—
Which having said, she cover'd up her face.

And, as he left her, sank in bitter prayer,—
If prayer that may be term'd which comes to all,
That sudden gushing of our vain despair,
When none but God can hear or heed our call;

And the wreck'd soul feels, in its helpless hour,
Where only dwells full mercy with full power.

And he came home, a crush'd and humbled wretch;
 Whom when she saw, she but this comfort found,
In her kind arms that shrinking form to catch,
 Which tenderly about his neck she wound,
As in the first proud days of love and trust,
E're yet his reckless head was bow'd in dust;

And they departed to a distant shore;
 But wheresoe'er they dwelt, however lone,
Shame, like a marble statue at his door,
 Flung her 'thwart shadow o'er his threshold stone;
Still darken'd all their daylight hours, and kept
Cold watch above them even while they slept.

And there was no more love between these two!
 It died not in the shock of that dark hour—
Such shocks destroy not love, whose purple hue
 Fades rather like some autumn-wither'd flower,
Which day by day along the ruin'd walk
We see—then miss it from the sapless stalk;

And, while it fadeth, oft with gentle hand
 Doth memory turn to life's dark journal-book
And, passing foul misdeeds, intently stand
 On its first page of glorious hope to look;

Weeping she reads,—and, seeing all so fair,
Pleads hard for what we *are*, by what we *were!*

So through that hour love lived; and, though in part
'Twas one of most unutterable pain,
It had its sweetness too, and told her heart
All she could do, and all she could sustain;
The holy love of woman buoy'd her up,
And God gave strength to drink the bitter cup.

But when, as days crept on, she saw him still
Less grateful than abash'd beneath her eye,
And studying not how best to banish ill,
But what he might conceal and what deny,
Her soul revolted, and conceived a scorn,
Sinful and harsh, although of virtue born.

And oft she pray'd, with earnestness and pain,
That heaven would bid that proud contempt depart,
And wept to find the prayer and effort vain,
Though it was breath'd in agony of heart—
Vain as the murmur of "Thy will be done,"
Breathed by the death-bed of an only son!

For when her children err'd (as children will)
A sickening terror smote her heart with fears,
And scarce she measured the degree of ill,
Or made indulgence for their tender years;
They were HIS children; and the chance of shame
Kept watch for those who bore that father's name

And, thinking thus, reproof would take a tone
So strangely passionate, severe, and wild,—
So deeply altered,—so unlike her own,—
It stung and terrified her startled child,
Whose innate sense of justice seemed to show
Him over-chidden, being chidden so.

And then a gush of mother's love would swell
Her grieving heart,—and she would fondly press
The young offending head she loved so well
Close to her own, with many a soft caress,
Whose reconciling sweetness all in vain
Stopp'd her boy's tears, while her's ran down like rain.

The world (which still pronounces from the show
Of outward things) whisper'd and talk'd of this;
Erring and obstinate, its crowds ne'er knew
How much in judging they may judge amiss,
Or how much agony and broken peace
May lie beneath the seeming of caprice!

But he, her husband (for he was not dull,)
Saw through these workings of a troubled mind,
And, that her cup of sorrow might be full,
He taunted her with words and looks unkind,
Which with a patient bowing of the heart
She took—like one resolved to do her part.

And years stole on (for years go by like days,
Leaving but scatter'd hours to mark their course,)
And brightness faded from that lady's gaze,
And her cheek hollow'd, and her step lost force,
Till it was plain to even a careless eye
That she was doom'd, before her time, to die.

She died, as she had lived, her secret soul
Shut from the sweet communion of true friends;
Her words, though not her thoughts, she could control,
And still with calm respect his name she blends:
They all stood round her whom she call'd her own,
And saw her die—yet was that death-bed lone!

But in its darkest hour her thoughts were stirr'd
And something falter'd from her dying tongue,
Mournful and tender—half pronounced, half heard—
For which *he* was too base—his boys too young;
So, whatsoe'er the warning faintly given,
It lay between her parting soul and Heaven.

He wept for her—ah! who would *not* have wept
To see that worn face in its pallid shroud,
Proving how much she suffer'd ere she slept

At peace for ever! Violent and loud
Was the outbreaking of his sudden grief,
And, like all feelings in that heart, 'twas brief.

And something strange pass'd o'er his soul instead,
When thinking upon her whom he had lost,
Almost like a *relief* that she was dead:—
She, whose high nature scorn'd his fault the most,
And show'd it least,—had vanish'd from the earth,
And none could check his sin, or shame his mirth.

So he return'd to many an evil way,
Like one who strays when guiding light is gone;
And mid the profligate, miscall'd "the gay,"
Crept to a slippery place—his tale half known—
Ill look'd on, yet endured—the useful tool
Of every bolder knave, or richer fool.

And his two sons in careless beauty grew,
Like wild flowers in his path: he mark'd them not,
Nor reck'd he what they needed, learnt, or knew,
Or what might be on earth their future lot;
But they died young—which is a thought of rest!—
Unscorn'd, untempted, undefiled—so best.

THE CREOLE GIRL.

Elle etait de ce monde, ou les plus belles choses
Ont le pire destin ;
Et Rose, elle a vecu ce que vivent les Roses,
L'espace d'un matin !

SHE came to England from the island clime
Which lies beyond the far Atlantic wave ;
She died in early youth—before her time—
"Peace to her broken heart, and virgin grave!"

She was the child of Passion, and of Shame,
English her father, and of noble birth ;
Though too obscure for good or evil fame,
Her unknown mother faded from the earth.

And what that fair West Indian did betide,
None knew but he, who least of all might tell,—
But that she lived, and loved, and lonely died,
And sent this orphan child with him to dwell.

Oh ! that a fair, an innocent young face
Should have a poison in its looks alone,

To raise up thoughts of sorrow and disgrace
 And shame most bitter, although not its own!

Cruel were they who flung that heavy shade
 Across the life whose days did but begin;
Cruel were they who crush'd her heart, and made
 Her youth pay penance for *his* youth's wild sin;

Yet so it was;—among her father's friends
 A cold compassion made contempt seem light,
But, in "the world," no justice e'er defends
 The victims of their tortuous wrong and right:—

And "moral England," striking down the weak,
 And smiling at the vices of the strong,
On her, poor child! her parent's guilt would wreak,
 And that which was her grievance, made her wrong.

The world she understood not; nor did they
 Who made that world,—her, either, understand;
The very glory of her features' play
 Seem'd like the language of a foreign land;

The shadowy feelings, rich and wild and warm,
 That glow'd and mantled in her lovely face,—

The slight full beauty of her youthful form,
  Its gentle majesty, its pliant grace,—

The languid lustre of her speaking eye,
  The indolent smile of that bewitching mouth,
(Which more than all betray'd her natal sky,
  And left us dreaming of the sunny South,)—

The passionate variation of her blood,
  Which rose and sank, as rise and sink the waves,
With every change of her most changeful mood,
  Shock'd sickly Fashion's pale and guarded slaves.

And so in this fair world she stood alone,
  An alien 'mid the ever-moving crowd,
A wandering stranger, nameless and unknown
  Her claim to human kindness disallow'd.

But oft would Passion's bold and burning gaze,
  And Curiosity's set frozen stare,
Fix on her beauty in those early days,
  And coarsely thus her loveliness declare!

Which she would shrink from, as the gentle plant,
  Fern-leaved Mimosa folds itself away;
Suffering and sad;—for easy 'twas to daunt
  One who on earth had no protecting stay.

And often to her eye's transparent lid
  The unshed tears would rise with sudden start,

And sink again, as though by Reason chid,
Back to their gentle home, her wounded heart;

Even as some gushing fountain idly wells
Up to the prison of its marble side,
Whose power the mounting wave forever quells,—
So rose her tears—so stemm'd by virgin pride.

And so more lonely each succeeding day,
As she her lot did better understand,
She lived a life which had in it decay,
A flower transplanted to too cold a land,—

Which for a while gives out a hope of bloom,
Then fades and pines, because it may not feel
The freedom and the warmth which gave it room
The beauty of its nature to reveal.

For vainly would the heart accept its lot,
And rouse its strength to bear avow'd contempt,
Scorn *will* be felt as scorn—deserved or not—
And from its bitter spell none stand exempt

There is a basilisk power in human eyes
When they would look a fellow-creature down,
Neath which the faint soul fascinated lies,
Struck by the cold sneer and the with'ring frown.

But one there was among the cruel crowd,
Whose nature *half* rebell'd against the chain,

Which fashion flung around him ; though too proud
To own that slavery's weariness and pain.

Too proud ; perhaps too weak ; for Custom still
Curbs with an iron bit the souls born free ;
They start and chafe, yet bend them to the will
Of this most nameless ruler,—so did he.

And even unto *him* the worldly brand
Which rested on her, half her charm effaced ;
Vainly all pure and radiant did she stand,—
Even unto *him* she was a thing disgraced.

Had she been early doom'd a cloister'd nun,
To Heaven devoted by an holy vow—
His union with that poor deserted one
Had seem'd not *more* impossible than now.

He *could* have loved her—fervently and well ;
But still the cold world with its false allure,
Bound his free liking in an icy spell,
And made its whole foundation insecure.

But not like meaner souls, would he, to prove
A vulgar admiration, her pursue ;
For though his glance after her would rove,
As something beautiful, and strange, and new

They were withdrawn if but her eye met his,
Or, for an instant if their light remain'd,
They soften'd into gentlest tenderness,
As asking pardon that his look had pain'd.

And she was nothing unto him,—nor he
  Aught unto her; but each of each did dream
In the still hours of thought, when we are free
  To quit the real world for things which seem.

When in his heart Love's folded wings would stir,
  And bid his youth choose out a fitting mate,
Against his will his thoughts roam'd back to her,
  And all around seem'd blank and desolate.

When, in his worldly haunts, a smother'd sigh
  Told he had won some lady of the land,
The dreaming glances of *his* earnest eye
  Beheld far off the Creole orphan stand;

And to the beauty by his side he froze,
  As though she were not fair, nor he so young,
And turn'd on her such looks of cold repose
  As check'd the trembling accents of her tongue,

And bid her heart's dim passion seek to hide
  Its gathering strength, although the task be pain,
Lest she become that mock to woman's pride—
  A wretch that loves unwoo'd, and loves in vain.

So in his heart she dwelt,—as one may dwell
  Upon the verge of a forbidden ground;
And oft he struggled hard to break the spell
  And banish her, but vain the effort found;

For still along the winding way which led
  Into his inmost soul, unbidden came
Her haunting form,—and he was visited
  By echoes soft of her unspoken name,

Through the long night, when those we love *seem* near,
  However cold, however far away,
Borne on the wings of floating dreams, which cheer
  And give us strength to meet the struggling day.

And when in twilight hours *she* roved apart,
  Feeding her love-sick soul with visions fair,
The shadow of *his* eyes was on her heart,
  And the smooth masses of his shining hair

Rose in the glory of the evening light,
  And, where she wander'd glided, evermore,
A star which beam'd upon her world's lone night
  Where nothing glad had ever shone before.

But vague and girlish was that love,—no hope,
  Even of familiar greeting, ever cross'd
Its innocent, but, oh! most boundless scope;
  She loved him,—and she knew her love was lost.

She gazed on him, as one from out a bark,
  Bound onward to a cold and distant strand,
Some lovely bay, some haven fair may mark,
  Stretching far inward to a sunnier land;

Who, knowing he must still sail on, turns back
To watch with dreaming and most mournful eyes
The ruffling foam which follows in his track,
Or the deep starlight of the shoreless skies.

Oh! many a hopeless love like this may be,—
For love will live that never looks to win·
Gems rashly lost in Passion's stormy sea,
Not to be lifted forth when once cast in!

PART II

So time roll'd on, till suddenly that child
Of southron clime and feelings, droop'd and pined;
Her cheek wax'd paler, and her eye grew wild,
And from her youthful form all strength declined.

'Twas then I knew her; late and vainly call'd
To "minister unto a mind diseased,"—
When on her heart's faint sickness all things pall'd,
And the deep inward pain was never eased:

Her step was always gentle, but at last
It fell as lightly as a wither'd leaf
In autumn hours; and wheresoe'er she pass'd
Smiles died away, she look'd so full of grief.

And more than ever from that world, where still
Her father hoped to place her, she would shrink;
Loving to be alone, her thirst to fill
From the sweet fountain where the dreamers drink.

One eve, beneath the acacia's waving bough,
Wrapt in these lonely thoughts she sate and read;
Her dark hair parted from her sunny brow,
Her graceful arm beneath her languid head;

And droopingly and sad she hung above
The open page, whereon her eyes were bent,
With looks of fond regret and pining love;
Nor heard my step, so deep was she intent.

And when she me perceived, she did not start,
But lifted up those soft dark eyes to mine,
And smiled, (that mournful smile which breaks the heart!)
Then glanced again upon the printed line.

"What readest thou?" I ask'd. With fervent gaze,
As though she would have scann'd my inmost soul,
She turn'd to me, and, as a child obeys
The accustom'd question of revered control,

She pointed to the title of that book,
(Which, bending down, I saw was "Coralie,")
Then gave me one imploring piteous look,
And tears, too long restrain'd, gush'd fast and free.

It was a tale of one, whose fate had been
Too like her own to make that weeping strange;
Like her, transplanted from a sunnier scene;
Like her, all dull'd and blighted by the change.

No further word was breathed between us two;—
No confidence was made to keep or break;—
But since that day, which pierced my soul quite thro',
My hand the dying girl would faintly take,

And murmur, as its grasp (ah! piteous end!)
Return'd the feeble pressure of her own,
"Be with me to the last,—for thou, dear friend,
Hast all my struggles, all my sorrow known!"

She died!—The pulse of that untrammell'd heart
Fainted to stillness. Those most glorious eyes
Closed on the world where she had dwelt apart
And her cold bosom heaved no further sighs.

She died!—and no one mourn'd, except her sire,

Who for a while look'd out with eyes more dim;
Lone was her place beside his household fire,
Vanish'd the face that ever smiled on him.

And no one said to him—"Why mournest thou?"
Because she was the unknown child of shame;
(Albeit her mother better kept the vow
Of faithful love, than some who keep their fame.)

Poor mother, and poor child!—unvalued lives!
Wan leaves that perish'd in obscurest shade!
While round me still the proud world stirs and strives,
Say, Shall I weep that ye are lowly laid?

Shall *I* mourn for ye? No!—and least for thee,
Young dreamer, whose pure heart gave way before
Thy bark was launch'd upon Love's stormy sea,
Or treachery wreck'd it on the farther shore.

Least, least of all for thee! Thou art gone hence?
Thee never more shall scornful looks oppress,
Thee the world wrings not with some vain pretence,
Nor chills thy tears, nor mocks at thy distress.

From man's injustice, from the cold award
Of the unfeeling, thou hast pass'd away;

Thou 'rt at the gates of light where angels guard
Thy path to realms of bright eternal day.

There shall thy soul its chains of slavery burst,
There, meekly standing before God's nigh throne,
Thou'lt find the judgments of our earth reversed,
And answer for no errors but thine own.

TWILIGHT.

It is the twilight hour,
The daylight toil is done,
And the last rays are departing
Of the cold and wintry sun.
It is the time when Friendship
Holds converse fair and free.
It is the time when children
Dance round the mother's knee.
But my soul is faint and heavy,
With a yearning sad and deep,
By the fireside lone and dreary
I sit me down and weep!
Where are ye, merry voices,
Whose clear and bird-like tone,
Some other ear now blesses,
Less anxious than my own?
Where are ye, steps of lightness,
Which fell like blossom-showers?

Where are ye, sounds of laughter,
  That cheer'd the pleasant hours?
Thro' the dim light slow declining,
  Where my wistful glances fall,
I can see your pictures hanging
  Against the silent wall;—
They gleam athwart the darkness,
  With their sweet and changeless eyes,
But mute are ye, my children!
  No voice to mine replies.
Where are ye? Are ye playing
  By the stranger's blazing hearth;
Forgetting, in your gladness,
  Your old home's former mirth?
Are ye dancing? Are ye singing?
  Are ye full of childish glee?
Or do your light hearts sadden
  With the memory of me?
Round whom, oh! gentle darlings,
  Do your young arms fondly twine,
Does she press you to *her* bosom
  Who hath taken you from mine?
Oh! boys, the twilight hour
  Such a heavy time hath grown,—
It recalls with such deep anguish
  All I used to call my own,—
That the harshest word that ever
  Was spoken to me there,
Would be trivial—would be *welcome*—
  In this depth of my despair!
Yet no! Despair shall sink not,
  While Life and Love remain,—

Tho' the weary struggle haunt me,
And my prayer be made in vain:
Tho' at times my spirit fail me,
And the bitter tear-drops fall,
Tho' my lot be hard and lonely,
Yet I hope—I hope thro' all!

When the mournful Jewish mother
Laid her infant down to rest,
In doubt, and fear, and sorrow,
On the water's changeful breast;
She knew not what the future
Should bring the sorely-tried:
That the High Priest of her nation,
Was the babe she ought to hide.
No! in terror wildly flying,
She hurried on her path:
Her swoln heart full to bursting
Of woman's helpless wrath;
Of that wrath so blent with anguish,
When we seek to shield from ill
Those feeble little creatures
Who *seem* more helpless still!
Ah! no doubt in such an hour,
Her thoughts were harsh and wild
The fiercer burned her spirit,
The more she loved her child;
No doubt, a frenzied anger
Was mingled with her fear,
When that prayer arose for justice
Which God hath sworn to hear.

He heard it! From His Heaven,
  In its blue and boundless scope,
He saw that task of anguish,
  And that fragile ark of hope;
When she turn'd from that lost infant,
  Her weeping eyes of love,
And the cold reeds bent beneath it—
  His angels watch'd above!
She was spared the bitter sorrow
  Of her young child's early death,
Or the doubt where he was carried
  To draw his distant breath;
She was call'd his life to nourish
  From the well-springs of her heart,
God's mercy re-uniting
  Those whom man had forced apart!

Nor was *thy* woe forgotten,
  Whose worn and weary feet
Were driven from thy homestead,
  Through the red sand's parching heat;
Poor Hagar! scorn'd and banish'd,
  That another's son might be
Sole claimant on that father,
  Who felt no more for thee.
Ah! when thy dark eye wander'd,
  Forlorn Egyptian slave!
Across that lurid desert,
  And saw no fountain wave,—
When thy southern heart, despairing,
  In the passion of its grief,
Foresaw no ray of comfort,

No shadow of relief;
But to cast the young child from thee,
That thou might'st not *see* him die,
How sank thy broken spirit—
But the Lord of Hosts was nigh!
He (He, too oft forgotten,
In sorrow as in joy)
Had will'd they should not perish—
The outcast and her boy:
The cool breeze swept across them
From the angel's waving wing,—
The fresh tide gush'd in brightness
From the fountain's living spring,—
And they stood—those two—forsaken
By all earthly love or aid,
Upheld by God's firm promise,
Serene and undismay'd!
And thou, Nain's grieving widow!
Whose task of life seem'd done,
When the pale corse lay before thee
Of thy dear and only son;
Though Death, that fearful shadow,
Had veil'd his fair young eyes,
There was mercy for thy weeping,
There was pity for thy sighs!
The gentle voice of Jesus,
(Who the touch of sorrow knew)
The grave's cold claim arrested
E'er it hid him from thy view;
And those loving orbs re-open'd
And knew thy mournful face,—

And the stiff limbs warm'd and bent them
  With all life's moving grace,—
And his senses dawn'd and waken'd
  From the dark and frozen spell,
Which death had cast around him
  Whom thou didst love so well;
Till, like one return'd from exile
  To his former home of rest,
Who speaks not while his mother
  Falls sobbing on his breast;
But with strange bewilder'd glances
  Looks round on objects near,
To recognise and welcome
  All that memory held dear,—
Thy young son stood before thee
  All living and restored,
And they who saw the wonder
  Knelt down to praise the Lord!

The twilight hour is over!
  In busier homes than mine
I can see the shadows crossing
  Athwart the taper's shine;
I hear the roll of chariots
  And the tread of homeward feet,
And the lamps' long rows of splendour
  Gleam through the misty street.
No more I mark the objects
  In my cold and cheerless room;
The fire's unheeded embers
  Have sunk—and all is gloom;
But I know where hang your pictures

Against the silent wall,
And my eyes turn sadly towards them,
Tho' I hope—I hope thro' all.
By the summons to that mother,
Whose fondness fate beguiled,
When the tyrant's gentle daughter
Saved her river-floating child ;—
By the sudden joy which bounded
In the banish'd Hagar's heart,
When she saw the gushing fountain
From the sandy desert start ;—
By the living smile which greeted
The lonely one of Nain,
When her long last watch was over
And her hope seem'd wild and vain
By all the tender mercy
God hath shown to human grief,
When fate or man's perverseness
Denied and barr'd relief,—
By the helpless woe which taught me
To look to him alone,
From the vain appeals for justice
And wild efforts of my own,—
By thy light—thou unseen future,
And thy tears—thou bitter past,
I will hope—tho' all forsake me.
In His mercy to the last !

THE BLIND MAN'S BRIDE.

When first, beloved, in vanish'd hours
  The blind man sought thy love to gain,
They said thy cheek was bright as flowers
  New freshen'd by the summer rain:
They said thy movements, swift yet soft,
  Were such as make the winged dove
Seem, as it gently soars aloft,
  The image of repose and love.

They told me, too, an eager crowd
  Of wooers praised thy beauty rare
But that thy heart was all too proud
  A common love to meet or share.
Ah! thine was neither pride nor scorn,
  But in thy coy and virgin breast
Dwelt preference, not of PASSION born,
  The love that hath a holier rest!

Days came and went;—thy step I heard
  Pause frequent, as it pass'd me by:—
Days came and went;—thy heart was stirr'd
  And answer'd to my stifled sigh!
And thou didst make a humble choice,

Content to be the blind man's bride,
Who loved thee for thy gentle voice,
And own'd no joy on earth beside.

And well by that sweet voice I knew
(Without the happiness of sight)
Thy years, as yet, were glad and few,
Thy smile, most innocently bright:
I knew how full of love's own grace
The beauty of thy form must be;
And fancy idolized the face
Whose loveliness I might not see!

Oh! happy were those days, beloved!
I almost ceased for light to pine
When thro' the summer vales we roved,
Thy fond hand gently link'd in mine.
Thy soft "Good night" still sweetly cheer'd
The unbroken darkness of my doom;
And thy "Good morrow, love," endear'd
Each sunrise that return'd in gloom!

At length, as years roll'd swiftly on,
They spoke to me of Time's decay—
Of roses from thy smooth cheek gone,
And ebon ringlets turn'd to gray.
Ah! then I *bless'd* the sightless eyes
Which could not feel the deepening shade,
Nor watch beneath succeeding skies
Thy withering beauty faintly fade.

I saw no paleness on thy cheek,
No lines upon thy forehead smooth,—

But still the BLIND MAN heard thee *speak*
  In accents made to bless and soothe.
Still he could feel thy guiding hand
  As thro' the woodlands wild we ranged,—
Still in the summer light could stand,
  And know thy HEART and VOICE unchanged.

And still, beloved, till life grows cold,
  We'll wander 'neath a genial sky,
And only know that we are old
  By counting happy years gone by:
For thou to *me* art still as fair
  As when those happy years began,—
When first thou cam'st to sooth and share
  The sorrows of a sightless man!

Old Time, who changes all below,
  To wean men gently for the grave,
Hath brought us no increase of woe,
  And leaves us all he ever gave:
For I am still a helpless thing,
  Whose darken'd world is cheer'd by thee—
And thou art she whose beauty's spring
  The blind man vainly yearn'd to see!

THE WIDOW TO HER SON'S BETROTHED.

Ah, cease to plead with that sweet cheerful voice,
Nor bid me struggle with a weight of woe,
Lest from the very tone that says "rejoice"
A double bitterness of grief should grow;
Those words from THEE convey no gladdening thought,
No sound of comfort lingers in their tone,
But by their means a haunting shade is brought
Of love and happiness forever gone!

My son!—alas, hast thou forgotten *him*,
That thou art full of hopeful plans again?
His heart is cold—his joyous eyes are dim,—
For him THE FUTURE is a word in vain!
He never more the welcome hours may share,
Nor bid Love's sunshine cheer our lonely home,—
How hast thou conquer'd all the long despair
Born of that sentence—*He is in the tomb?*

How can thy hand with cheerful fondness press
The hands of friends who still on earth may stay—
Remembering *his* most passionate caress
When the LONG PARTING summon'd him away?
How can'st thou keep from bitter weeping, while
Strange voices tell thee thou art brightly fair—
Remembering how *he* loved thy playful smile,
Kiss'd thy smooth cheek, and praised thy burnish'd hair?

How can'st thou laugh? How can'st thou warble songs?
How can'st thou lightly tread the meadow-fields,
Praising the freshness which to spring belongs,
And the sweet incense which the hedge-flower yields?
Does not the many-blossom'd spring recall
Our pleasant walks through cowslip-spangled meads,—
The violet-scented lanes—the warm south-wall,
Where early flow'rets rear'd their welcome heads?

Does not remembrance darken on thy brow
When the wild rose a richer fragrance flings—
When the caressing breezes lift the bough,
And the sweet thrush more passionately sings;—

Dost thou not, then, lament for him whose form
  Was ever near thee, full of earnest grace?
Does not the sudden darkness of the storm
  Seem luridly to fall on Nature's face?

It does to ME! The murmuring summer breeze,
  Which thou dost turn thy glowing cheek to meet,
For *me* sweeps desolately through the trees,
  And moans a dying requiem at my feet!
The glistening river which in beauty glides,
  Sparkling and blue with morn's triumphant light,
All lonely flows, or in its bosom hides
  A broken image lost to human sight!

But THOU!—Ah! turn thee not in grief away;
  I do not wish *thy* soul as sadly wrung—
I know the freedom of thy spirit's play,
  I know thy bounding heart is fresh and young:
I know corroding Time *will* slowly break
  The links which bound most fondly and most fast,
And Hope *will* be Youth's comforter, and make
  The long bright Future overweigh the Past.

Only, when full of tears I raise mine eyes
  And meet *thine* ever full of smiling light,
I feel as though thy vanished sympathies
  Were buried in HIS grave, where all is night;
And when beside our lonely hearth I sit,
  And thy light laugh comes echoing to my ear,

I wonder how the waste of mirth and wit
Hath still the power thy widow'd heart to cheer!

Bear with me yet! Mine is a harsh complaint!
And thy youth's innocent light-heartedness
Should rather soothe me when my spirit's faint
Than seem to mock my age's lone distress.
But oh! the tide of grief is swelling high,
And if so soon forgetfulness must be—
If, for the DEAD, thou hast no further sigh,
Weep for his Mother!—Weep, young Bride, for ME!

THE DYING HOUR.

"Te teneam moriens, deficiente manu."

OH! watch me; watch me still
Thro' the long night's dreary hours,
Uphold by thy firm will
Worn Nature's sinking powers!

While yet *thy* face is there
(The loose locks round it flying,)
So young, and fresh, and fair,
I feel not I am dying!

Stoop down, and kiss my brow!
  The shadows round me closing
Warn me that dark and low
  I soon shall be reposing.

But while those pitying eyes
  Are bending thus above me,
In vain the death-dews rise,—
  Thou dost regret and love me!

Then watch me thro' the night,
  Thro' my broken, fitful slumbers;
By the pale lamp's sickly light
  My dying moments number!

Thy fond and patient smile
  Shall soothe my painful waking;
Thy voice shall cheer me while
  The slow gray dawn is breaking!

The battle-slain, whose thirst
  No kindly hand assuages,
Whose low faint farewell burst
  Unheard, while combat rages,—

The exiled, near whose bed
  Some vision'd form seems weeping
Whose steps shall never tread
  The land where he lies sleeping,—

The drown'd, whose parting breath
  Is caught by wild winds only,—
Theirs is the bitter death,
  Beloved, for they die lonely!

But thus, tho' rack'd, to lie,
  Thou near, tho' full of sadness,
Leaves still, e'en while I die,
  A lingering gleam of gladness!

I feel not half my pain
  When to mine thy fond lip presses,—
I warm to life again
  Beneath thy soft caresses!

Once more, oh! yet once more
  Fling, fling thy white arms round me,
As oft in days of yore
  Their gentle clasp hath bound me;

And hold me to that breast
  Which heaves so full with sorrow—
Who knows where I may rest
  In the dark and blank to-morrow?

Ah! weep not—it shall be
  An after-thought to cheer thee,
That while mine eyes *could* see,
  And while mine ears could hear thee—

Thy voice and smile were still
  The spells on which I doated,
And thou, through good and ill,
  To me and mine devoted!

And calmly by my tomb,
  When the low bright day declineth,
And athwart the cypress gloom
  The mellow sunset shineth,—

Thou'lt sit and think of Him,
  Who, of Heaven's immortal splendor,
Had a dream on earth, though dim,
  In thy love so pure and tender,—

Who scarcely feels thy touch,—
  Whom thy voice can rouse no longer,—
But whose love on earth was such,
  That only death was stronger.

Yes, sit, but not in tears!
  Thine eyes in faith uplifting,
From thy lot of changeful years,
  To the Heaven where nought is shifting

From this world, where all who love
  Are doomed alike to sever,
To the glorious realms above,
  Where they dwell in peace for ever!

And then such hope shall beam
  From the grave where I lie sleeping,
This bitter hour shall seem
  Too vague and far for weeping—

And grief—ah! hold me now!
  My fluttering pulse is failing,—
The death-dews chill my brow,—
  The morning light is paling!

I seek thy gaze in vain,—
  Earth reels and fades before me,
I die--but feel no pain,--
  Thy sweet face shining o'er me.

I CANNOT LOVE THEE.

I CANNOT love thee, tho' my soul
Be one which all good thoughts control;
Altho' thy eyes be starry bright,
And the gleams of golden light
Fall upon thy silken hair,
And thy forehead, broad and fair;
Something of a cold disgust,
(Wonderful, and most unjust,)
Something of a sullen fear
Weighs my heart when thou art near;
And my soul, which cannot twine
Thought or sympathy with thine,
With a coward instinct tries
To hide from thy enamor'd eyes.
Wishing for a sudden blindness
To escape those looks of kindness;
Sad she folds her shivering wings
From the love thy spirit brings,
Like a chained thing, caress'd
By the hand it knows the best,
By the hand which, day by day,
Visits its imprison'd stay,
Bringing gifts of fruit and blossom

From the green earth's plenteous bosom;
All but that for which it pines
In those narrow close confines,
With a sad and ceaseless sigh—
Wild and winged Liberty!

Can it be, no instinct dwells
In th' immortal soul, which tells
That thy love, oh! human brother.
Is unwelcome to another?
Can the changeful wavering eye,
Raised to thine in forced reply,—
Can the cold constrained smile,
Shrinking from thee all the while,
Satisfy thy heart, or prove
Such a likeness of true love?

Seems to me, that I should guess
By what a world of bitterness,
By what a gulf of hopeless care,
Our two hearts divided were:
Seems to me that I should know
All the dread that lurk'd below,
By the want of answer found
In the voice's trembling sound
By the unresponsive gaze;
By the smile which vainly plays,
In whose cold imperfect birth
Glows no fondness, lives no mirth;
By the sigh, whose different tone
Hath no echo of thine own;

By the hand's cold clasp, which still
Held as not of its free will,
Shrinks, as it for freedom yearn'd;—
That my love was unreturn'd.

When thy tongue (ah! woe is me!)
Whispers love-vows tenderly,
Mine is shaping, all unheard,
Fragments of some withering word,
Which, by its complete farewell,
Shall divide us like a spell!
And my heart beats loud and fast,
Wishing that confession past;
And the tide of anguish rises,
Till its strength my soul surprises,
And the reckless words, unspoken,
Nearly have the silence broken,
With a gush like some wild river,—
"Oh! depart, depart for ever!"

But my faltering courage fails,
And my drooping spirit quails;
So sweet-earnest looks thy smile
Full of tenderness the while,
And with such strange pow'r are gifted
The eyes to which my own are lifted;
So my faint heart dies away,
And my lip can nothing say,
And I long to be alone,—
For I weep when thou art gone!

Yes, I weep, but then my soul,
Free to ponder o'er the whole,

Free from fears which check'd its thought,
And the pain thy presence brought,
Whispers me the useless lie,—
"For thy love he will not die,
Such pity is but vanity."
And I bend my weary head
O'er the tablets open spread,
Whose fair pages me invite
All I dared not say to write;
And my fingers take the pen,
And my heart feels braced again
With a resolute intent;—
But, ere yet that page be sent,
Once I view the written words
Which must break *thy* true heart's chords;
And a vision, piercing bright,
Rises on my coward sight,
Of thy fond hand, gladly taking
What must set thy bosom aching;
While too soon the brittle seal
Bids the page the worst reveal,
Blending in thy eager gaze—
Scorn, and anguish, and amaze.

Powerless, then, my hand reposes
On the tablet which it closes,
With a cold and shivering sense
Born of Truth's omnipotence:
And my weeping blots the leaves,
And my sinking spirit grieves.
Humbled in that bitter hour
By very consciousness of power!

What am I, that I should be
Such a source of woe to thee?
What am I, that I should dare
Thus to play with thy despair,
And persuade myself that thou
Wilt not bend beneath the blow?

Rather should my conscience move
Me to think of this vain love,
Which my life of peace beguiles,
As a tax on foolish smiles,
Which—like light not meant for one
Who, wandering in the dark alone,
Hath yet been tempted by its ray
To turn aside and lose his way—
Binds me, by their careless sin,
To take the misled wanderer in.

And I praise thee, as I go,
Wandering, weary, full of woe,
To my own unwilling heart;
Cheating it to take thy part
By rehearsing each rare merit
Which thy nature doth inherit.
To myself their list I give,
Most prosaic, positive:—
How thy heart is good and true,
And thy face most fair to view;
How the powers of thy mind
Flatterers in the wisest find,
And the talents God hath given
Seem as held in trust for Heaven;

Laboring on for noble ends,—
Steady to thy boyhood's friends,—
Slow to give, or take, offence,—
Full of earnest eloquence,—
Hopeful, eager, gay of cheer,—
Frank in all thy dealings here,—
Ready to redress the wrong
Of the weak against the strong,—
Keeping up an honest pride
With those the world hath deified,
But gently bending heart and brow
To the helpless and the low ;—
How, in brief, there dwells in thee
All that's generous and free,
All that may most aptly move
My Spirit to an answering love.

But in vain the tale is told;
Still my heart lies dead and cold,
Still it wanders and rebels
From the thought that thus compels,
And refuses to rejoice
Save in unconstrained choice.

Therefore, when thine eyes shall read
This, my book, oh take thou heed!
In the dim lines written here,
All shall be explained and clear;
All my lips could never speak
When my heart grew coward-weak,
All my hand could never write,

Tho' I planned it day and night,—
All shall be at length confest,
And thou'lt forgive,—and let me rest!
None but thou and I shall know
Whose the doom, and whose the woe;
None but thou and I shall share
In the secret printed there;
It shall be a secret still,
Tho' all look on it at will;
And the eye shall read in vain
What the heart cannot explain.
Each one, baffled in his turn,
Shall no more its aim discern,
Than a wanderer who might look
On some wizard's magic book,
Of the darkly-worded spell
Where deep-hidden meanings dwell.
Memory, fancy, they shall task
This sad riddle to unmask,—
Or, with bold conjectural fame,
Fit the pages with a name;—
But nothing shall they understand,
And vainly shall the stranger's hand
Essay to fling the leaves apart,
Which bears MY message to THY heart!

THE POET'S CHOICE.

'Twas in youth, that hour of dreaming;
Round me, visions fair were beaming,
Golden fancies, brightly gleaming,
                    Such as start to birth
When the wandering restless mind,
Drunk with beauty, thinks to find
Creatures of a fairy kind
                    Realized on Earth!

Then, for me, in every dell
Hamadryads seem'd to dwell
(They who die, as Poet's tell,
                    Each with her own tree;)
And sweet mermaids, low reclining,
Dim light through their grottos shining,
Green weeds round their soft limbs twining,
                    Peopled the deep Sea.

Then, when moon and stars were fair,
Nymph-like visions fill'd the air,
With blue wings and golden hair
                    Bending from the skies;
And each cave by echo haunted

In its depth of shadow granted,
Brightly, the Egeria wanted,
To my eager eyes.

But those glories pass'd away;
Earth seem'd left to dull decay,
And my heart in sadness lay,
Desolate, uncheer'd;
Like one wrapt in painful sleeping,
Pining, thirsting, waking, weeping,
Watch thro' Life's dark midnight keeping,
Till THY form appear'd!

THEN my soul, whose erring measure
Knew not where to find true pleasure,
Woke and seized the golden treasure
Of thy human love;
And, looking on thy radiant brow,
My lips in gladness breathed the vow
Which angels, not more fair than thou,
Have register'd above.

And now I take my quiet rest,
With my head upon thy breast,
I will make no further quest
In Fancy's realms of light;
Fay, nor nymph, nor winged spirit,
Shall my store of love inherit;
More thy mortal charm doth merit
Than dream, however bright.

And my soul, like some sweet bird
Whose song at summer eve is heard,

When the breeze, so lightly stirr'd,
Leaves the branch unbent,—
Sits and all triumphant sings,
Folding up her brooding wings,
And gazing out on earthly things
With a calm content.

THE GERMAN STUDENT'S LOVE-SONG.

"Ich liebe dich!"

By the rush of the Rhine's broad stream,
Down whose rapid tide
We sailed as in some sweet dream
Sitting side by side;
By the depth of its clear blue wave
And the vine-clad hills,
Which gazed on its heart and gave
Their tribute rills;

By the mountains, in purple shade,
And those valleys green
Where our bower of rest was made,
By the world unseen;
By the notes of the wild free bird,
Singing over-head,

When naught else in the sunshine stirr'd
  Round our flowery bed;

    By these, and by Love's power divine,
    I have no thought but what is thine!

By the glance of thy radiant eyes,
  Where a glory shone
That was half of the summer skies
  And half their own;
By the light and yet fervent hold
  Of thy gentle hand.—
(As the woodbines the flowers unfold
  With their tender band;)

By thy voice when it breathes in song,
  And the echo given
By lips that to Earth belong,
  Float up to Heaven;
By the gleams on thy silken hair
  At the sunset hour,
And the breadth of thy forehead fair
  With its thoughtful power;

    By these, and by Love's soul divine,
    I have no hope but what is thine!

By the beauty and stillness round
  When the lake's lone shore
Scarce echoed the pleasant sound
  Of the distant oar;
By the moonlight which softly fell

On all objects near,
And thy whisper seemed like a spell
In thy Lover's ear;

By the dreams of the restless past,
And the hope that came
Like sunshine in shadow cast
With thy gentle name;
By the beat of thy good true heart
Where pure thoughts have birth;
By thy tears when Fate bade us part,
And thy smiles of mirth;

By these, and by Love's power divine,
I have no hope but what is thine!

By the gloom of those holy fanes
Where the light stream'd through
Dim orange and purple panes
On the aisles below;
By the ruin'd and roofless wall
Of that castle high,
With its turrets so gray and tall
In the clear blue sky;

By beauty, because its light
Should thy portion be,
And whatever is fair and bright
Seems a part of thee;
And by darkness and blank decay
Because they tell

What the world would be, THOU away,
Whom I love so well ;

By these, and by Love's power divine,
My heart, my soul, my life, are thine!

THE HUNTING HORN OF CHARLEMAGNE.

Among other relics preserved in the Cathedral at Aix-la-Chapelle is the ivory hunting-horn of Charlemagne. It is massive and heavy, and the attempt of the guide to sound it (for the amusement of tourists and strangers) is singularly unsuccessful, the note produced being the most faint and lugubrious which it is possible to conceive.

SOUND not the horn!—the guarded relic keep :
A faithful sharer of its master's sleep:
His life it gladden'd—to his life belong'd,—
Pause—ere thy lip the royal dead hath wrong'd.
Its weary weight but mocks thy feeble hand ;
Its desolate note, the shrine wherein we stand.
Not such the sound it gave in days of yore,
When that rich belt a monarch's bosom wore,—
Not such the sound! Far over hill and dell
It waked the echoes with triumphant swell ;
Heard midst the rushing of the torrent's fall
From castled crag to roofless ruin'd hall,

Down the ravine's precipitous descent,
Thro' the wild forest's rustling boughs it went,
Upon the lake's blue bosom linger'd fond,
And faintly answer'd from the hills beyond :

Pause !—the free winds that joyous blast have borne :—
Dead is the hunter !—silent be the horn !

Sound not the horn ! Bethink thee of the day
When to the chase an Emperor led the way ;
In all the pride of manhood's noblest prime,
Untamed by sorrow, and untired by time,
Life's pulses throbbing in his eager breast,
Glad, active, vigorous,—who is now at rest :—
How he gazed around him with his eagle eye,
Leapt the dark rocks that frown against the sky,
Grasp'd the long spear, and curb'd the panting steed,
(Whose fine nerves quiver with his headlong speed
At the wild cry of danger smiled in scorn,
And firmly sounded that re-echoing horn !

Ah ! let no touch the ivory tube profane
Which drank the breath of *living* Charlemagne ;
Let not like blast by meaner lips be blown,
But by the hunter's side the horn lay down !

Or, following to his palace, dream we now
Not of the hunter's strength or forest bough,

But woman's love! HER offering this, perchance,—
This, granted to each stranger's casual glance,
This, gazed upon with coldly curious eyes,
Was giv'n with blushes, and received with sighs
We see her not;—no mournful angel stands
To guard her love-gift from our careless hands
But fancy brings a vision to our view—
A woman's form, the trusted and the true:
The strong to suffer, tho' so weak to dare,
Patient to watch thro' many a day of care,
Devoted, anxious, generous, void of guile,
And with her whole heart's welcome in her smile;
Even such I see! Her maidens, too, are there,
And wake, with chorus sweet, some native air;
But tho' her proud heart holds her country dear,
And tho' she loves those happy songs to hear,
She bids the tale be hush'd, the harp be still,
For one faint blast that dies along the hill.
Up, up, she springs; her young head backward thrown;
"He comes! my hunter comes!—Mine own—mine own!"

She loves, and she is loved—her gift is worn—
'Tis fancy, all!—And yet—lay down the horn!

LOVE—life—what are ye?—since to love and live
No surer record to our times can give!
Low lies the hero now, whose spoken name

Could fire with glory, or with love inflame;
Low lies the arm of might, the form of pride,
And dim tradition dreameth by his side.
Desolate stands those painted palace-halls,
And gradual ruin mines the massy walls,
Where frank hearts greeted many a welcome
guest,
And loudly rang the beaker and the jest;—
While *here*, within this chapel's narrow bound,
Whose frozen silence startles to the sound
Of stranger voices ringing thro' the air,
Or faintly echoes many a humble prayer;
Here, where the window, narrow arch'd, and
high,
With jealous bars shuts out the free blue sky,—
Where glimmers down, with various-painted
ray,
A prison'd portion of God's glorious day,—
Where never comes the breezy breath of morn,
Here, mighty hunter, feebly wakes thy horn!

THE FAITHFUL FRIEND.

"Coming through the churchyard here, I espied a young man who had flung himself down on the grave to weep, and who ever and anon repeated, with most passionate lamentations, "O, friend! faithful friend!" Respecting his grief, I passed on, marvelling as I went what manner of man he had been who slept under that stone."—*Letters of a Tourist.*

O, FRIEND! whose heart the grave doth shroud
From human joy or woe,
Know'st thou who wanders by thy tomb,
With footsteps sad and slow?
Know'st thou whose brow is dark with grief?
Whose eyes are dim with tears?
Whose restless soul is sinking
With its agony of fears?
Whose hope hath failed, whose star hath sunk,
Whose firmest trust deceived,
Since, leaning on thy faithful breast,
He loved and he believed?
'Tis I!—Return and comfort me,
For old remembrance sake.—

From the long silence of the tomb—
  The cheerless tomb—awake!
I listen—all is still as death—
  No welcome step is nigh,—
I call thee, but thou answerest not
  The grave hath no reply!
But mournfully the strange bright sun
  Shines on thy funeral stone,
And sadly, in the cypress bough,
  The wild wind makes her moan.

When we were young, and cheerfully
  The promised future glow'd,
I little thought to stand alone
  By this thy last abode;
I little thought, in early days,
  O generous and kind!
That THOU, the first, shouldst quit the earth
  And leave me, wreck'd, behind.

Thine was the pure unjealous love!
  I know they told us then
That Genius' gifts divided me
  From dull and common men;
That thou wert slow to science;
  That the chart and letter'd page
Had in them no deep spell whereby
  Thy spirit to engage;
But rather thou wouldst sail thy boat,
  Or sound thy bugle horn,
Or track the sportsman's triumph through
  The fields of waving corn,

Than o'er the pond'rous histories
  Of other ages bend,
Or dwell upon the sweetest page
  That poet ever penn'd:
And it was true! Our minds were cast
  As pleased the will of Heaven,
And different powers unto me,
  And unto thee, were given!
No trick of talent deck'd thy speech
  And glorified thy youth,—
Its simple spell of eloquence
  Lay in its earnest truth;
Nor was the gladsome kindliness
  Which brighten'd on thy brow,
The beauty which in fiction wins
  Love's fond romantic vow;
But gazing on thine honest face,
  Intelligently bold,
Oft have I doubted of the gifts
  Which men so precious hold,—
Wit, learning, wealth, seem'd overprized
  Since thou, dear friend, couldst be
So closely knit unto my heart
  By thy simplicity.

The worldly-wise may sneer at this,
  And scorn thee, if they will,—
Thy judgment was not sharpen'd by
  The cunning of their skill;
No deep and calculating thoughts
  Lay buried in thy breast,

To chill and vex thy honest heart,
  And startle it from rest;
No dream of cold philosophy,
  To make thee doubt and sigh,
And fawn and flatter half thy kind,
  And pass the others by!
And there thou liest forgotten—
  Thou faithful friend, and true—
Thy resting-place beneath the cold
  Damp shadow of the yew;
And quietly within the tomb's
  Dark precints wert thou laid,
As a faded leaf unnoticed drops
  Within the forest shade.

How should the world have tears for thee!
  The world hath nothing lost—
No parent's high ambitious hope
  THY early death hath crost;
No sculptured falsehood gives to fame
  Thy monumental stone,—
From the glory of our Senate-house,
  No orator is gone:
Science hath lost no well-known name,—
  No soldier's heart shall bound,
Linking old England's victories
  With that inglorious sound;
No jealous and tomb-trampling foe
  Shall find it worth his while,
With a false history of thy acts,
  Thy country to beguile;

No mercenary hand in haste
  Prepare the letter'd tome,
And publicly reveal the fond
  Small weaknesses of Home;
Nor some vainglorious friend (who yet
  Hath lov'd thee to the last)
Permit all men to buy and sell
  His records of the past;
Nor give thy living letters up,
  Nor print thy dying words;
Nor sweep with sacrilegious hand
  Affection's holy chords;
Nor with a frozen after-thought
  Dissect thy generous heart,
And count each pulse that bid thy blood
  Gush with a quicker start.

No! Blest OBSCURITY was thine!
  In sacred darkness dwells
The mem'ry of THY last fond looks
  And faltering farewells;
And none shall drag thy actions forth,
  For Slander or for Praise,
To that broad light which never glowed
  Round thy unnoticed days.
At times a recollected jest,
  Or snatch of merry song,
Which was so *thine*, that still to thee
  Its ringing notes belong,
To boon companions back again
  Thy image may recall,—
But lightly sits thy memory,

Oh Faithful Friend, on all !
The old house still hath echoes glad ;
Tho' silent be thy voice,
Thy empty place at bed and boa
Forbids not to rejoice !
Still with its white and gleaming sail,
By stranger's launch'd to float
Across the blue lake in the sun,
Glides on thy little boat ;
Thy steed another rider backs,–
Thy dogs new masters find,
But I,—*I* mourn thy absence still
Thou generous and kind :
Since I have lost thy pleasant smile,
And voice of ringing mirth,
A silence and a darkness seems
Come down upon the earth ;
A weight sits heavy on my heart,
And clogs my weary feet,
For, wander where I will, *thy* glance
I never more shall meet,
I cannot knit my soul again ;
My thoughts are wide astray
When others by my side would wile
An hour or two away ;
My door flings wide to welcome in
Some less familiar face,
And my heart struggles hard to fill
Thy ever vacant place ;
But all in vain ! Dim thoughts of THEE
Across my bosom steal,
And still, the louder mirth around.

The lonelier I feel;
Yea, even that should make me proud,
The laurel wreath of Fame
But brings me back our early days,
And the echo of thy name;
But brings me back thy cheerful smile,
When yet a careless boy,
Mine was the toil, but thou didst share
The glory and the joy;
And bright across the awarded prize
Thy kind eye answer'd mine,
As full of triumph and delight
As though that prize were thine.
Yes! all is vain! I want not Wit,
I want not Learning's power,
I want THY hand, I want THY smile
To pass the cheerless hour;
I want thy earnest, honest voice,
Whose comfort never fail'd;
I want thy kindly glance, whose light
No coldness ever veil'd:
I feel at every turn of life
Thy loss hath left me lone,
And I mourn the friend of boyhood's years
The friend for ever gone!

THE WINTER'S WALK.

* Written after walking with Mr. Rogers

MARK'D—as the hours should be, Fate bids us
spend
With one illustrious, or a cherish'd friend—
Rich in the value of that double claim,
Since Fame allots the friend a Poet's name,—
My " Winter's Walk" asserts its right to live
Amongst the brightest thoughts my life can give.
And leaves a track of light on Memory's way
Which oft shall gild the future Summer's day.

Gleam'd the red sun athwart the misty haze
Which veil'd the cold earth from its loving gaze,
Feeble and sad as Hope in Sorrow's hour,—
But for THY soul it still had warmth and power;
Not to its cheerless beauty wert thou blind,
To the keen eye of thy poetic mind
Beauty still lives, tho' nature's flow'rets die,
And wintry sunsets fade along the sky!
And naught escaped thee as we stroll'd along,
Nor changeful ray, nor bird's faint chirping song;
Bless'd with a fancy easily inspired,

All was beheld, and nothing unadmired;
Not one of all God's blessings giv'n in vain,
From the dim city to the clouded plain.

And many an anecdote of other times,
Good earnest deeds,—quaint wit,—and polished
rhymes,—
Many a sweet story of remembered years
Which thrilled the listening heart with unshed
tears,—
Unweariedly thy wi ling tongue rehearsed,
And made the hour seem brief as we conversed.

Ah! who can e'er forget, who once hath heard,
The gentle charm that dwells in every word
Of thy calm converse? In its kind allied
To some fair river's bright abundant tide,
Whose silver gushing current onward goes,
Fluent and varying; yet with such repose
As smiles even through the flashings of thy wi ;
In every eddy that doth ruffle it.
Who can forget, who at thy soc al board
Hath sat,—and seen the pictures richly stored,
In all their tints of glory and of gloom,
Brightening the precints of thy quiet room;
With busts and statues full of that deep grace
Which modern hands have lost the skill to trace,
(Fragments of beauty—perfect as thy song
On that sweet land to which they did belong,)
Th' exact and classic taste by thee displayed;
Not with a rich man's idle fond parade,
Not with the pomp of some vain connoisseur

Proud of his bargains, of his judgment sure,
But with the feelings kind and sad, of one
Who thro' far countries wandering hath gone,
And brought away dear keepsakes, to remind
His heart and home of all he left behind.

But wherefore these, in feeble rhyme recall?
Thy taste, thy wit, thy verse, are known to all;
Such things are for the World, and therefore doth
The World speak of them; loud, and nothing loth
To fancy that the talent stamped by Heaven
Is naught unless their echoed praise be given,
A worthless ore not yet allowed to shine,
A diamond darkly buried in its mine.
These are thy daylight qualities, whereon
Beams the full lustre of their garish sun,
And the keen point of many a famed reply
Is what they would not "willingly let die."
But by a holier light thy angel reads
The unseen records of more gentle deeds,—
And by a holier light thy angel sees
The tear oft shed for humble miseries,—
The alms dropp'd gently in the beggar's hand,
(Who in his daily poverty doth stand
Watching for kindness on thy pale calm brow,
Ignorant to whom he breathes his grateful vow.)
Th' indulgent hour of kindness stol'n away
From the free leisure of thy well-spent day,
For some poor struggling Son of Genius, bent
Under the weight of heart-sick discontent;

Whose prayer thou hearest, mindful o the schemes
Of thine own youth;—the hopes, the fever-dreams
Of Fame and Glory which seemed hovering then,
(Nor only *seemed*) upon thy magic pen;
And measuring not how much beneath thine own
Is the sick mind thus pining to be known,
But only what a wealth of hope lies hushed
As in a grave,—when men like these are chrushed!

And by that light's soft radiance *I* review
Thy unpretending kindness, calm and true,
Not to me only,—but in bitterest hours
To one whom Heaven endowed with varied flowers;
To one who died, e'er yet my childish heart
Knew what Fate meant, or Slander's fabled dart!
Then was the laurel green upon his brow,
And they could flatter then, who judge him now,
Who, when the fickle breath of fortune changed,
With equal falsehood held their love estranged;
Nay, like mean wolves, from whelp-hood vainly nurst,
Tore at the easy hand that fed them first.
Not so didst THOU the ties of friendship break—
Not so didst THOU the saddened man forsake;
And when at length he laid his dying head

On the hard rest of his neglected bed,
He found,—(Tho' few or none around him came
Whom he had toiled for in his hour of Fame;—
Though by his Prince, unroyally forgot,
And left to struggle with his altered lot;—)
By sorrow weakened,—by disease unnerved,—
Faithful at least the friend he had *not* served:
For the same voice essayed that hour to cheer,
Which now sounds welcome to his grandchild's
ear;
And the same hand, to aid that Life's decline,
Whose gentle clasp so late was linked in mine!

THE REPRIEVE.

Suggested by a beautiful little Picture painted by J. R. Herbert, Esq., representing, in the foreground, a Woman pleading with a Warrior, and, in the back ground, preparations for an Execution.

A MOMENT since, he stood unmoved—alone,
Courage and thought on his resolved brow;
But hope is quivering in the broken tone,
Whose bitter anguish seems to shake him
now:
Her light foot woke no echo as it came,
The rustling robe her sudden swiftness told;
She pleads for one who dies a death of shame;
She pleads—for love and agony are bold.

"Oh! hear me, thou, who in the sunshine's glare
So calmly waitest till the warning bell
Shall of the closing hour of *his* despair
In gloomy notes of muffled triumph tell.
Let him not die! Avenging Heaven is just;
Thine, a like fate in after years may be:
Thy forfeit head may gasping bite the dust,
While those *thou* lovest, plead in vain for thee!
Thou smilest sternly: thou could'st well brave death;
Hast braved it often on the tented field.
So fought *my* hero on th' ensanguined heath,
With desperate strength, that knew not how to yield:
But oh! the death whose punctual hour is set,
And waited for mid lingering thoughts of pain;
Where no excitement bids the heart forget,
And skill and courage are alike in vain;
Who shall find strength for *that*?—Oh! man, to whom
Fate, chance, or what thou wilt, hath given this hour—
Upon whose will depends his dreaded doom—
Doth it not awe thee, thinking of thy power?
In the wide battle's hot and furious rage,
Where the mix'd banners flutter to and fro,
Where all alike the desperate combat wage,
One of the thousand swords may pierce him through:
But, now, *his life is in thy single hand:*

To thee the strange and startling power is given—
And thou shalt answer for this day's command
When ye stand face to face in God's own Heaven.
Bear with me! pardon me this sudden start!
My words are bitter, for my heart is sore!
And oh! dark soldier of the iron heart,
Fain would I learn the speech should touch thee more!
He hath a mother—age hath dimm'd her sight—
But when his quick returning step comes nigh,
She smiles, as though she saw a sudden light,
And turns to bless him with a stiffled sigh.
When to *her* arms a lonely wretch I go,
And she doth ask for him, the true and brave,
While on her cheek faint smiles of welcome glow,
How shall I answer 'he is in the grave!'
He hath a little son--a mirthful boy,
Whose coral lips with ready smiles are curl'd;
Wilt thou quench all the spring-time of his joy,
And leave him orphan in a friendless world?
Hast *thou* no children?—Do no visions come,
When the low night-wind through the poplar grieves--
Echoes of farewell voices—sounds of home—
For which thy busy day no leisure leaves?
Some one doth love thee—some one thou dost love—

(For such the blessed lot of all on earth,)
Some one to whom thy thoughts oft fondly rove,
The sharer of thy sorrows and thy mirth;
Who with dim weeping eyes, and thoughts that burn,
Sees thy proud form lead forth th' embattled host;
To whom 'a victory' speaks of *thy* return—
And 'a defeat' means only *thou* art lost!
If such there be, (and on thy helm-worn brow
Sternness, not cruelty, doth seem to reign,)
Think it is she, who kneels before thee now,
Her heart which bursts with agony of pain.

"Hark!—'Tis the warning stroke—his hour is come—
I hear the bell slow clanging on the air—
I hear the beating of the muffled drum—
Thou hast a moment yet to save and spare!
Oh! when returning to thy native land,
Greeted with grateful tears and loud acclaim;
While gazing on thy homeward march they stand,
And smiling children shout thy welcome name:
How wilt thou bear the joyous village chimes,
Whose ringing peals remind thee of to-day—
Will not my image haunt thee at those times?
And my hoarse desperate voice seem yet to pray?
When the long term of bloody toil is past,
And the hush'd trumpet calls no more to arms—
Will not *his* death thy tranquil brow o'ercast,

And rob that peaceful hour of half its charms?
When thy child's mother bends thy lip to press,
And her true hand lies clasp'd within thine own—
Will her low voice have perfect power to bless,
Remembering *me*, the widow'd and the lone?
When they embrace thee—when they wel come thee——
By all my hopes of Heaven, thy brow relents!
Oh! sign the paper—let his life go free—
Give it me quick!"—
"What ho! Raise her—the woman faints!"

THE FORSAKEN.

Suggested by an Italian picture, of a dying girl, to whom the lute is being played.

It is the music of her native land,—
The airs she used to love in happier days;
The lute is struck by some young gentle hand,
To soothe her spirit with remember'd lays.

But her sad heart is wandering from the notes,
Her ear is fill'd with an imagined strain;
Vainly the soften'd music round her floats,
The echo it awakes is all of pain!

The echo it awakes, is of a voice
Which never more her weary heart shall cheer;
Fain would she banish it, but hath no choice,
Its vanish'd sound still haunts her shrinking ear,—

Still haunts her with its tones of joy and love,
Its memories of bitterness and wrong,
Bidding her thoughts thro various changes rove,—
Welcomes, farewells, and snatches of wild song.

Why bring her music? She had half forgot
How left, how lonely, how oppress'd she was;
Why, by these strains, recal her former lot,
The depth of all her suffering, and its cause?

Know ye not what a spell there is in sound?
Know ye not that the melody of *words*
Is nothing to the power that wanders round,
Giving vague language to harmonious chords?

Oh! keep ye silence! *He* hath sung to her
And from that hour—(faint twilight, sweet and dim,
When the low breeze scarce made the branches stir)—
Music hath been a memory of HIM!

Chords which the wandering fingers scarcely touch
When they would seek for some forgotten song,—

Stray notes which have no certain meaning, such
As careless hands unthinkingly prolong,—

Come unto HER, fraught with a vivid dream
Of love, in all its wild and passionate strength,—
Of sunsets, glittering on the purple stream,—
Of shadows, deepening into twilight length,—

Of gentle sounds, when the warm world lay hush'd
Beneath the soft breath of the evening air,—
Of hopes and fears, and expectations crush'd,
By one long certainty of blank despair!

Bear to the sick man's couch the fiery cup,
Pledged by wild feasters in their riotous hours,
And bid his parch'd lips drink the poison up,
As tho' its foam held cool refreshing powers,—

Lift some poor wounded wretch, whose writhing pain
Finds soothing only in an utter rest,
Forth in some rude-made litter, to regain
Strength for his limbs and vigor for his breast;—

But soothe ye not that proud forsaken heart
With strains whose sweetness maddens as they fall;
Untroubled let her feverish soul depart—
Not long shall memory's power its might enthral·

Not long,—tho' balmy be the summer's breath;
 In the deep stillness of its golden light,
A shadowy spirit sits, whose name is DEATH,
 And turns, what was all beauty, into blight;

And she, before whose sad and dreaming eye
 Visions of by-gone days are sweeping on,
In her unfaded youth shall drooping die,
 Shut from the glow of that Italian sun:

Then let the organ's solemn notes prolong
 Their glory round the silence of her grave,
Then let the choral voices swell in song
 And echo through the chancel and the nave!

For then her heart shall ache not at the sound,
 Then the faint fever of her life shall cease;
Silence, unbroken, calm, shall reign around,
 And the long restless shall be laid at peace.

THE VISIONARY PORTRAIT

As by his lonely hearth he sate,
 The shadow of a welcome dream
Pass'd o'er his heart,—disconsolate
 His home did seem;
Comfort in vain was spread around,
For something still was wanting found.

Therefore he thought of one who might
  Forever in his presence stay ;
Whose dream should be of him by night,
  Whose smile should be for him by day ;
And the sweet vision, vague and far,
Rose on his fancy like a star.

" Let her be young, yet not a child,
  Whose light and inexperienced mirth
Is all too winged and too wild
  For sober earth,—
Too rainbow-like such mirth appears,
And fades away in misty tears.

" Let youth's fresh rose still gently bloom
  Upon her smooth and downy cheek,
Yet let a shadow, not of gloom,
  But soft and meek,
Tell that *some* sorrow she hath known,
Tho' not a sorrow of her own.

" And let her eyes be of the gray,
  The soft gray of the brooding dove,
Full of the sweet and tender ray
  Of modest love;
For fonder shows that dreamy hue
Than lustrous black or heavenly blue.

"Let her be full of quiet grace,
  No sparkling wit with sudden glow
Bright'ning her purely chisell'd face
  And placid brow ;

Not radiant to the *stranger's* eye,—
A creature easily pass'd by;

"But who, once seen, with untold power
For ever haunts the yearning heart,
Raised from the crowd that self-same hour
To dwell apart,
All sainted and enshrined to be
The idol of our memory!

"And oh! let Mary be her name—
It hath a sweet and gentle sound
At which no glories dear to fame
Come crowding round,
But which the dreaming heart beguiles
With holy thoughts and household smiles.

"With peaceful meetings, welcomes kind,
And love, the same in joy and tears,
And gushing intercourse of mind
Thro' faithf l years;
Oh! dream of something half divine,
Be real--be mortal—and be mine!"

THE PICTURE OF SAPPHO.

Thou! whose impassion'd face
The Painter loves to trace,
Theme of the Sculptor's art and Poet's story--
How many a wand'ring thought
Thy loveliness hath brought
Warming the heart with its imagined glory!

Yet, was it History's truth,
That tale of wasted youth,
Of endless grief, and Love forsaken pining?
What wert thou, thou whose woe
The old traditions show
With Fame's cold light around thee vainly shining?

Didst thou inded sit there
In languid lone despair—
Thy harp neglected by thee idly lying—
Thy soft and earnest gaze
Watching the lingering rays
In the far west, where summer-day was dying—

While with low rustling wings
Among the quivering strings
The murmuring breeze faint melody was making
As though it wooed thy hand
To strike with new command,
Or mourn'd with thee because thy heart was breaking?

Didst thou, as day by day
Roll'd heavily away,
And left thee anxious, nerveless, and dejected,
Wandering thro' bowers beloved—
Roving where *he* had roved—
Yearn for his presence, as for one expected?

Didst thou, with fond wild eyes
Fix'd on the starry skies,

Wait feverishly for each new day to waken—
   Trusting some glorious morn
   Might witness his return,
Unwilling to believe thyself forsaken?

   And when conviction came,
   Chilling that heart of flame,
Didst thou, O saddest of earth's grieving daughters!
   From the Leucadian steep
   Dash, with a desperate leap,
And hide thyself within the whelming waters!

   Yea, in their hollow breast
   Thy heart at length found rest!
The ever-moving waves above thee closing—
   The winds, whose ruffling sigh
   Swept the blue waters by,
Disturb'd thee not!—thou wert in peace reposing!

   Such is the tale they tell!
   Vain was thy beauty's spell—
Vain all the praise thy song could still inspire
   Though many a happy band
   Rung with less skilful hand
The borrowed love-notes of thy echoing lyre.

   FAME, to thy breaking heart
   No comfort could impart,
In vain thy brow the laurel wreath was wearing,
   One grief and one alone
   Could bow thy bright head down—
Thou wert a WOMAN, and wert left despairing!

THE SENSE OF BEAUTY.

Spirit! who over this our mortal Earth,
Where naught hath birth
Which imperfection doth not some way dim,
Since Earth offended Him—
Thou who unseen, from out thy radiant wings
Dost shower down light o'er mean and common things;
And, wandering to and fro,
Through the condemn'd and sinful world dost go,
Haunting that wilderness, the human heart,
With gleams of glory that too soon depart,
Gilding both weed and flower;—
What is thy birth divine? and whence thy mighty power?

The Sculptor owns thee! On his high pale brow
Bewild'ring images are pressing now;
Groups whose immortal grace
His chisel ne'er shall trace,
Though in his mind the fresh creation glows;
High forms of godlike strength,
Or limbs whose languid length

The marble fixes in a sweet repose!
At thy command,
His true and patient hand
Mould's the dull clay to Beauty's richest line,
Or with more tedious skill,
Obedient to thy will,
By touches imperceptable and fine,
Works slowly day by day
The rough-hewn block away.
Till the soft shadow of the bust's pale smile
Wakes into *statue-life* and pays the assiduous toil!

Thee, the young Painter knows,—whose fervent eyes,
O'er the blank waste of canvass fondly bending,
See fast within its magic circle rise
Some pictured scene, with colors softly blending,—
Green bowers and leafy glades,
The old Arcadian shades,
Where thwarting glimpses of the sun are thrown,
And dancing nymphs and shepherds one by one
Appear to bless his sight
In Fancy's glowing light,
Peopling that spot of green Earth's flowery breast
With every attitude of joy and rest.

Lo! at his pencil's touch steals faintly forth
(Like an uprising star in the cold north)
Some face which soon shall glow with beauty's fire:

Dim seems the sketch to those who stand around,
Dim and uncertain as an echoed sound,
But oh! how bright to him, whose hand *thou*
dost inspire!

Thee, also, doth the dreaming Poet hail,
Fond comforter of many a weary day—
When through the clouds his Fancy's car can
sail
To worlds of radiance far, *how* far, away!
At thy clear touch (as at the burst of light
Which Morning shoots along the purple hills,
Chasing the shadows of the vanish'd night,
And silvering all the darkly gushing rills,
Giving each waking blossom, gemm'd with dew,
Its bright and proper hue;)—
He suddenly beholds the chequered face
Of this old world in its young Eden grace!
Disease, and want, and sin, and pain, are not—
Nor homely and familiar things:—man's lot
Is like aspirations—bright and high;
And even in the haunting thought that man
must die,
His dream so changes from its fearful strife,
Death seems but fainting into purer life!

Nor only these thy presence woo,
The less inspired own thee too!
Thou hast thy tranquil source
In the deep well-springs of the human heart,
And gushest with sweet force
When most imprison'd; causing tears to start

In the worn citizen's o'erwearied eye,
As, with a sigh,
At the bright close of some rare holiday,
He sees the branches wave, the waters play—
And hears the clock's far distant mellow chime
Warn him a busier world reclaims his time!

Thee, Childhood's heart confesses,—when he sees
The heavy rose-bud crimson in the breeze,
When the red coral wins his eager gaze,
Or the warm sunbeam dazzles with its rays,
Thee, through his varied hours of rapid joy,
The eager Boy,—
Who wild across the grassy meadow springs,
And still with sparkling eyes
Pursues the uncertain prize,
Lured by the velvet glory of its wings!

And so from youth to age—yea, till the end—
An unforsaking, unforgetting friend,
Thou hoverest round us! And when all is o'er,
And Earth's most loved illusions please no more,
Thou stealest gently to the couch of Death;
There, while the lagging breath
Comes faint and fitfully, to usher nigh
Consoling visions from thy native sky,
Making it sweet to die!
The sick man's ears are faint—his eyes are dim—
But his heart listens to the Heavenward hymn,
And his soul sees—in lieu of that sad band,
Who come with mournful tread

To kneel about his bed,--
God's white-robed angels, who around him stand.
And waive his Spirit to "the Better Land!"

So, living,—dying,--still our hearts pursue
That loveliness which never met our view;
Still to the last the ruling thought will reign,
Nor deem one feeling given—was giv'n *in vain*.
For it may be, our banish'd souls recall
In this, their earthly thrall,
(With the sick dreams of exiles,) that far world
Whence angels once were hurl'd;
Or it may be, a faint and trembling sense,
Vague, as permitted by Omnipotence,
Foreshows the immortal radiance round us shed
When the Imperfect shall be perfected!
Like the chain'd eagle in his fetter'd might,
Straining upon the Heavens his wistful sight,
Who toward the upward glory fondly springs
With all the vain strength of his shivering wings,—
So chain'd to earth, and baffled—yet so fond
Of the pure sky which lies so far beyond,
We make *the attempt to soar* in many a thought
Of Beauty born, and into Beauty wrought;
Dimly we struggle onwards:—who shall say
Which glimmering light leads nearest to the day?

THE MOTHER'S HEART.

When first thou camest, gentle, shy, and fond,
My eldest-born, first hope, and dearest trea-
sure,
My heart received thee with a joy beyond
All that it yet had felt of earthly pleasure;
Nor thought that *any* love again might be
So deep and strong as that I felt for thee.

Faithful and true, with sense beyond thy years,
And natural piety that lean'd to Heaven;
Wrung by a harsh word suddenly to tears,
Yet patient to rebuke when justly given—
Obedient—easy to be reconciled—
And meekly cheerful—such wert thou, my child!

Not willing to be left; still by my side
Haunting my walks, while summer-day was
dying:—
Nor leaving in thy turn; but pleased to glide
Thro' the dark room where I was sadly lying,
Or by the couch of pain, a sitter meek,
Watch the dim eye, and kiss the feverish cheek

O boy! of such as thou are oftenest made
  Earth's fragile idols; like a tender flower,
No strength in all thy freshness,—prone to fade,—
  And bending weakly to the thunder-shower,—
Still, round the loved, thy heart found force to bind,
And clung, like woodbine shaken in the wind!

Then THOU, my merry love;—bold in thy glee,
  Under the bough, or by the firelight dancing,
With thy sweet temper, and thy spirit free,
  Didst come, as restless as a bird's wing glancing,
Full of a wild and irrepressible mirth,
Like a young sunbeam to the gladden'd earth!

Thine was the shout! the song! the burst of joy!
  Which sweet from childhood's rosy lip resoundeth:
Thine was the eager spirit naught could cloy,
  And the glad heart from which all grief reboundeth;
And many a mirthful jest and mock reply,
Lurk'd in the laughter of thy dark-blue eye!

And thine was many an art to win and bless,
  The cold and stern to joy and fondness warming;
The coaxing smile;—the frequent soft caress;—
  The earnest tearful prayer all wrath disarming!
Again my heart a new affection found,
But thought that love with *thee* had reached its bound.

At length THOU camest: thou, the last and least;
Nick-named "The Emperor" by thy laughing brothers,
Because a haughty spirit swell'd thy breast,
And thou didst seek to rule and sway the others;
Mingling with every playful infant wile
A mimic majesty that made us smile:

And oh! most like a regal child wert thou!
An eye of resolute and successful scheming!
Fair shoulders—curling lip—and dauntless brow—
Fit for the world's strife, not for Poet's dreaming:
And proud the lifting of thy stately head,
And the firm bearing of thy conscious tread.

Different from both! Yet each succeeding claim,
I, that all other love had been forswearing,
Forthwith admitted, equal and the same;
Nor injured either, by this love's comparing
Nor stole a fraction for the newer call—
But in the Mother's Heart, found room for all

MAY-DAY, 1837.

MAY-DAY is come!—While yet the unwilling Spring
  Checks with capricious frown the opening year,
Onward, where bleak winds have been whispering,
  The punctual Hours their ancient playmate bear;
But those who long have look'd for thee, stand by,
  Like men who welcome back a friend bereaved,
And cannot smile, because his sadden'd eye
  Doth mutely tell them how his soul is grieved.
    Even thus *we* greet thine alter'd face to-day,
    Thou friend in mourning garb!—chill, melancholy May!

To thee the first and readiest smiles of Earth,
  Lovely with life renew'd, were always given,—
To thee belong'd the sunshine and the mirth
  Which bathed all Nature with a glow from Heaven,—
To thee the joy of Childhood's earnest heart,

His shouting song, and light elastic tread,
His brows high arch'd, and laughing lips apart,
Bright as the wreath that bound his rosy head:—
Thou wert of innocence the holiday,
Thou garlanded and glad!—thou ever-blooming May!

Yet will I not reproach thee for thy change:
Closed be the flower, and leafless be the tree!
Smile not as thou wert wont; but sad, and strange,
And joyless, let thy tardy coming be!
So shall I miss those infant voices less,
Calling each other through the garden bowers,
Meeting and parting in wild happiness,
Leading a light dance thro' the sunny hours;
Those little mirthful hearts, who, far away,
Breathe, amid cloud-capp'd hills, a yet more wintry May!

Ah, boys! your play-ground is a desert spot,
Revisited alone, and bathed with tears;
And where *ye* pass your May-day, knoweth not
The mother who hath watch'd your dawning years.
Mine is no more the joy to see ye come,
And deem each step hath some peculiar grace!
Yours is no more the mother's welcome home,
Smiling at each beloved, familiar face!
And I am thankful that this dreary May
Recalls not, save by name, that brighter, happier day!

I should have felt more mock'd, if there had been
  More peace and sunshine round me,—had the grove,
Clad in transparent leaves of tender green,
  Been full of murm'ring sounds of Nature's love;
I should have wept more bitterly beneath
  The frail laburnum trees, so faint and fair,—
I should have sicken'd at the lilac's breath,
  Thrown by the warm sun on the silent air;
    But now, with stern regret I wend my way—
    I know thee not,—thou cold and unfamiliar May!

TO THE LADY H. O.

Come o'er the green hills to the sunny sea!
  The boundless sea, that washeth many lands,
Where shells unknown to England, fair and free,
  Lie brightly scatter'd on the gleaming sands.
There, 'midst the hush of slumbering ocean's roar,
  We'll sit and watch the silver-tissued waves
Creep languidly along the basking shore,
  And kiss thy gentle feet, like Eastern slaves.

And we will take some volume of our choice,
  Full of a quiet poetry of thought,
And thou shalt read me, with thy plaintive voice,

Lines which some gifted mind hath sweetly
wrought;
And I will listen, gazing on thy face,
(Pale as some cameo on the Italian shell!)
Or looking out across the far blue space,
Where glancing sails to gentle breezes swell.

Come forth! The sun hath flung on Thetis'
breast
The glittering tresses of his golden hair;
All things are heavy with a noonday rest,
And floating sea-birds leave the stirless air.
Against the sky, in outlines clear and rude,
The cleft rocks stand, while sunbeams slant
between;
And lulling winds are murmuring thro' the wood,
Which skirts the bright bay with its fringe of
green.

Come forth! All motion is so gentle now,
It seems *thy* step alone should walk the
earth,—
Thy voice alone, the "ever soft and low,"
Wake the far-haunting echoes into birth.
Too wild would be Love's passionate store of
hope,
Unmeet the influence of his changeful power,—
Ours be companionship, whose gentle scope
Hath charm enough for such a tranquil hour.

And slowly, idly wandering, we will roam,
Where the high cliffs shall give us an ample
shade;

And watch the glassy waves, whose wrathful foam
  Hath power to make the seaman's heart afraid.
Seek thou no veil to shroud thy soft brown hair,--
  Wrap thou no mantel round thy graceful form;
The cloudless sky smiles forth as still and fair,
  As tho' earth ne'er could know another storm.

Come! Let not listless sadness make delay,—
  Beneath Heaven's light that sadness will depart;
And as we wander on our shoreward way,
  A strange, sweet peace shall enter in thine heart.
We will not weep, nor talk of vanish'd years,
  When, link by link, Hope's glittering chain was riven:
Those who are dead, shall claim from love no tears,—
  Those who have injured us, shall be forgiven.

Few have my summers been, and fewer thine;—
  Youth blighted is the weary lot of both:
To both, all lonely shows our life's decline,
  Both with old friends and ties have waxed wroth.
But yet we will not weep! The breathless calm
  Which lulls the golden earth, and wide blue sea,
Shall pour into our souls mysterious balm,
  And fill us with its own tranquility.

We will not mar the scene—we will not look
  To the veil'd future, or the shadowy past;
Seal'd up shall be sad Memory's open book,
  And childhood's idleness return at last!
Joy, with his restless, ever-fluttering wings,
  And Hope, his gentle brother,—all shall cease:
Like weary hinds that seek the desert springs,
  Our one sole feeling shall be peace—deep
    peace!

THE FALLEN LEAVES.

We stand among the fallen leaves,
  Young children at our play,
And laugh to see the yellow things
  Go rustling on their way:
Right merrily we hunt them down,
  The autumn winds and we,
Nor pause to gaze where snow-drifts lie,
  Or sunbeams gild the tree:
With dancing feet we leap along
  Where wither'd boughs are strown,
Nor past nor future checks our song—
  The present is our own.

We stand among the fallen leaves
  In youth's enchanted spring—
When Hope (who wearies at the last)

First spreads her eagle wing.
We tread with steps of conscious strength
Beneath the leafless trees,
And the color kindles in our cheek
As blows the winter breeze;
While, gazing towards the cold gray sky,
Clouded with snow and rain,
We wish the old year all past by,
And the young spring come again.

We stand among the fallen leaves
In manhood's haughty prime—
When first our pausing hearts begin
To love "the olden time;"
And, as we gaze, we sigh to think
How many a year hath pass'd
Since 'neath those cold and faded trees
Our footsteps wander'd last;
And old companions—now perchance
Estranged, forgot, or dead—
Come round us, as those autumn leaves
Are crush'd beneath our tread.

We stand among the fallen leaves
In our *own* autumn day—
And, tott'ring on with feeble steps,
Pursue our cheerless way.
We look not back—too long ago
Hath all we loved been lost;
Nor forward—for we may not live
To see our new hope cross'd:
But on we go—the sun's faint beam

A feeble warmth imparts—
Childhood without its joy returns-
The present fills our hearts !

THE AUTUMN WIND.

Hush, moaning autumn wind ! be still, be still !
Thy grieving voice forbiddeth hearts to rest ;
We hear thee sweeping down the lonely hill,
And mournful thoughts crowd o'er the human breast,
Why wilt thou haunt us, with thy voice unkind,
Sadd'ning the earth ? Hush, moaning autumn wind !

Toss not the branching trees so wildly high,
Filling the forest with thy dreary sound :
Without *thy* aid the hues of summer die,
And the sear leaves fall scatter'd to the ground.
Thou dost but hasten, needlessly unkind,
The winter's task, thou moaning autumn wind !

Sweep not through Ocean's caves with hollow roar,
Driving our fair ships to some rock-bound strand !
While the vex'd sea foams wrathful to the shore,
The seaman's wife looks shuddering from the land,

And widow'd hearts for many a year shall find
Death in thy voice, thou moaning autumn wind!

Round our calm dwellings, when our hearths are gay,
Roam not, oh howling Spirit of Despair!
As tho' thou wert a creature seeking prey,
And where the land look'd richest, found it there.
We have enough of memories unkind,
Without thy voice, thou moaning autumn wind!

Thee the sad mourner lists, and turns to weep,
In the blank silence of her lonely home;
The sick man hears, and starts from broken sleep,
And the night-wanderer sighs—compell'd to roam;
While the poor shiver, for *their* huts unkind
Bar thee not out, thou searching autumn wind!

Back to the barren hill and lonely glen!
Here let the wandering of thy echoes cease;
Sadly thou soundest to the hearts of men,—
Hush thy wild voice, and let the earth have peace;
Or, if *no* chain thy restless will can bind,
Sweep thro, the desert, moaning autumn wind.

THE TRYST.

I WENT, alone, to the old familiar place
Where we often met,—
When the twilight soften'd thy bright and radi
ant face
And the sun had set.
All things around seem'd whispering of the past,
With thine image blent—
Even the changeful spray which the torrent cast
As it downward went!
I stood and gazed with a sad and heavy eye
On the waterfall—
And with a shouting voice of agony
On thy name did call!

With a yearning hope, from my wrung and
aching heart
I call'd on thee—
And the lonely echoes from the rocks above
They answer'd me!
Glad and familiar as a household word
Was that cherish'd name—
But in that grieving hour, faintly heard,
'Twas not the same!

Solemn and sad, with a distant knelling cry,
On my heart it fell—
'Twas as if the word "Welcome" had been answer'd by
The word "FAREWELL!"

THE BANNER OF THE COVENANTERS.

At the Mareschal College at Aberdeen, among other valuable curiosities, they show one of the banners formerly belonging to the Covenanters; it is of white silk, with the motto, "Spe Expecto," in red letters; and underneath, the English inscription, "For Religion, King, and Kingdoms." The banner is much torn, but otherwise in good preservation.

HERE, where the rain-drops may not fall,
The sunshine doth not play,
Where the unfelt and distant breeze
In whispers dies away;
Here, where the stranger paces slow
Along the silent halls,
Why mutely art thou hanging thus
Against the massive walls?
Thou, that hast seen blood shed for thee—
That midst the battle-tide
Hast faintly lit the soldier's eye

With triumphs ere he died;
Bright banner, which hath witness'd oft
The struggles of the free,
Emblem of proud and holy hope,
Is this a place for *thee*?

Wake! wave aloft, thou banner!
Let every snowy fold
Float on our wild, unconquer'd hills,
As in the days of old:
Hang out, and give again to Death
A glory and a charm,
Where Heaven's pure dew may freshen thee,
And Heaven's pure sunshine warm.
Wake, wave aloft! I hear the silk
Low rustling on the breeze,
Which whistles through the lofty fir,
And bends the birchen trees;
I hear the tread of warriors arm'd
To conquer or to die;
Their bed or bier the heathery hill,
Their canopy the sky.

What, what is life or death to them?
They only feel and know
Freedom is to be struggled for,
With an unworthy foe—
Their homes—their hearths—the all for which
Their fathers, too, have fought,
And liberty to breathe the prayers
Their cradled lips were taught.

On, on they rush—like mountain streams
  Resistlessly they sweep—
On! those who live are heroes now—
  And martyrs those who sleep!
While still the snow-white Banner waves
  Above the field of strife,
With a proud triumph, as it were
  A thing of soul and life.

They stand—they bleed—they fall! they make
  One brief and breathless pause,
And gaze with fading eyes upon
  The standard of their cause;—
Again they brave the strife of death,
  Again each weary limb
Faintly obeys the warrior soul,
  Tho' earth's best hopes grow dim;—
The mountain-rills are red with blood,
  The pure and quiet sky
Rings with the shouts of those who win,
  The groans of those who die;
Taken—re-taken—raised again,
  But soil'd with clay and gore,
Heavily, on the wild free breeze,
  That Banner floats once more.

I hear the wail of women now:
  The dreadful day is done:
God's creatures wait to strive and slay
  Until to-morrow's sun:
I hear the heavy breathing of
  The weary ones who sleep,

The death-sob and the dying word,
  "The voice of them that weep;"
The half-choked grief of those who, while
  They stifle back their breath,
Scarce knew if what they watch be hush'd
  In slumber or in death;
While mournfully, as if it knew
  And felt for their despair,
The moon-lit Banner flaps and falls
  Upon the midnight air.

Morning! the glad and glorious light!
  The waking of God's earth,
Which rouses men to stain with gore
  The soil that gave them birth.
In the still sunshine sleeps the hill,
  The stream, the distant town;
In the still sunshine—clogg'd and stiff—
  The battle-flag hangs down.

Peace is in Heaven, and Heaven's good gifts,
  But war is amongst men—
Red blood is pouring on the hill,
  Wild shouts are in the glen;
'Tis past—they sink, they bleed, they fly—
  That faint, enfeebled host,
Right is not might—the Banner-flag,
  The victory, are lost!

Heaven's dew hath drunk the crimson drops
  Which on the heather lay,
The rills that were so red with gore,

Go sparkling on their way;
The limbs that fought, the hearts that swell'd,
Are crumbled into dust,
The souls which strove are gone to meet
The spirits of the just;
But that frail silken flag, for which,
And under which, they fought,
(And which e'en *now* retains its power
Upon the soul of thought,)
Survives—a tatter'd, senseless thing—
To meet the curious eye,
And wake a momentary dream
Of hopes and days gone by.

A momentary dream! oh! not
For *one* poor transient hour,
Not for a brief and hurried day
That flag exerts its power;
Full flashing on our dormant souls
The firm conviction comes,
That what our fathers did for *theirs*,
We could do for *our* homes.
We, *too*, could brave the giant arm
That seeks to chain each word,
And rule what form of prayer alone
Shall by our God be heard:
We, too, in triumph or defeat,
Could drain our heart's best veins,
While the good old cause of Liberty
For Church and State remains!

THE ROCK OF THE BETRAYED.

It was a Highland chieftain's son
  Gazed sadly from the hill:
And they saw him shrink from the autumn wind,
  As its blast came keen and chill.

His stately mother saw,—and spoke
  With the heartless voice of pride;
"'T is well I have a stouter son
  The border wars to ride."

His jealous brother saw, and stood,
  Red-hair'd, and fierce, and tall,
Muttering low words of fiendish hope
  To be the lord of all.

But sickly Allan heard them not,
  As he look'd o'er land and lea;
He was thinking of the sunny climes
  That lie beyond the sea.

He was thinking of the native land
  Whose breeze he could not bear,

Whose wild free beauty he must leave,
To breath a warmer air.

He was dreaming of his childhood's haunts,
And his grey-hair'd father's praise!
And the chance of death which hung so near
And darken'd his young days.

So he turn'd, and bade them both farewell,
With a calm and mournful smile;
And he spoke of dwelling far away,
But only for awhile.

And if a pang of bitter grief
Shot wildly through his heart,
No man heard Allan Douglass sigh,
Nor saw the tear-drop start:

For he left in Scotland none who cared
If e'er he should return,
In castle hall, or cottage low,
By river or by burn.

Only upon the heather brae
His quivering lip he press'd;
And clasp'd the senseless birchen tree,
And strain'd it to his breast;

Because the human heart is full
Of love that *must* be given,
However check'd, estranged, and chill'd,
To something under Heaven.

And these things had been friends to him
  Thro' a life of lonely hours—
The blue lake, and the waving birch,
  And the low broom's scented flowers.

* * * *

Twice had the snow been on the hills,
  And twice the soft spring rain,
When Allan Douglass bent his way
  To his native land again.

More healthful glow'd his hollow cheek,
  His step was firm and free,
And he brought a fair Italian girl,
  His bonny bride to be.

But darkly sneer'd his brother cold,
  When he saw that maiden fair,
"Is a foreign minion come to wed
  The Highland chieftain's heir?"

And darkly gloom'd the mother's brow
  As she said, "Am I so old,
That a stranger must so soon come here
  The castle keys to hold?"

Then spoke the young, Italian girl
  With a sweet and modest grace,
As she lifted up her soft black eyes
  And look'd them in the face:

"A stranger and an orphan comes
  To Allan's native land,

And she needs the mother's welcome smile,
 And the brother's friendly hand.

"Be thine! oh, stately lady—thine—
 The rule that thou dost crave,
For Allan's love is all I earn'd,
 And all I seek to have.

"And trust me, brother, tho' my words
 In foreign accents fall,
The *heart* is of no country born,
 And my heart will love you *all.*"

But vain the music of her tongue
 Against the hate they bore;
And when a babe her love had bless'd
 They hated her the more.

They hated her the more because
 That babe must be the heir,
And his dark and lovely eyes at times
 His mother's look would bear.

But lo! the keen cold winter came
 With many a bitter blast:
It pierc'd thro' sickly Allan's frame,
 He droop'd and died at last!

Oh! mournfully at early morn
 That young wife sat and wept,—
And mournfully, when day was done.
 To her widow'd couch she crept,—

And mournfully at noon she rock'd
  The baby on her knee;
"There is no pity in their hearts,
  My child, for thee and me.

"There was no pity in their hearts
  For him who is at rest:
How should they feel for his young son
  Who slumbers at my breast?"

The red-hair'd brother saw her tears,
  And said, "Nay, cease thy moan—
Come forth into the morning air,
  And weep no more alone!"

The proud step-mother chid her woe;—
  "Even for thy infant's sake
Go forth into the morning air,
  And sail upon the lake!"

There seem'd some feeling for her state;
  Their words were fair and mild;
Yet she shudder'd as she whisper'd low,
  "God shield me and my child!"

"Come!" said the dead Allan's brother stern,
  "Why dost thou tremble so?
"Come!"—and with doubt and fear perplex'd,
  The lady rose to go.

They glided over the glassy lake,
  'Till its lulling murmur smote,

With a death-like omen, to and fro',
  Against the heaving boat.

And no one spoke ;—that brother stil
  His face averted kept,
And the lady's tears fell fast and free
  O'er her infant as it slept.

The cold faint evening breeze sprang up
  And found them floating on ;
They glided o'er the glassy lake
  Till the day's last streak was gone—

Till the day's last streak had died away
  From the chill and purple strand,
And a mist was on the water's face
  And a damp dew on the land ;

Till you could not trace the living hue
  Of lip, or cheek, or eye,
But the outline of each countenance
  Drawn dark against the sky.

And all things had a ghastly look,
  An aspect strange and drear ;—
The lady look'd to the distant shore
  And her heart beat wild with fear.

* * * *

There is a rock whose jutting height
  Stands frowning o'er that lake,

Where the faintest call of the bugle horn
  The echo's voice will awake :—

And there the water lifts no wave
  To the breeze, so fresh and cool,
But lies within the dark rock's curve,
  Like a black and gloomy pool,

Its depth is great,—a stone thrown in
  Hath a dull descending sound,
The plummet hath not there been cast
  Which resting-place hath found.

And scatter'd firs and birch-trees grow
  On the summit, here and there—
Lonely and joylessly they wave,
  Like an old man's thin gray hair.

But not to nature's hand it owes
  Its mournfulness alone,
For vague tradition gives the spot
  A horror of its own.

The boatman doffs his cap beneath
  Its dark o'er hanging shade,
And whispers low its Gaelic name,—
  "The Rock of the Betray'd."

And when the wind, which never curls
  That pool, goes sweeping by,
Bending the firs and birchen trees
  With a low and moaning sigh,—

He'll tell you that the sound which comes
  So strange, and faint, and dim,
Is only heard at one set hour,
  And call'd "THE LADY'S HYMN."

WEEP NOT FOR HIM THAT DIETH.

" Weep ye not for the dead, neither bemoan him; but weep sore for him that goeth away, for he shall return no more, nor see his native country."—*Jeremiah*, xxii, 10.

WEEP not for him that dieth—
  For he sleeps, and is at rest;
And the couch whereon he lieth
  Is the green earth's quiet breast:
But weep for him who pineth
  On a far land's hateful shore,
Who wearily declineth
  Where ye see his face no more!

Weep not for him that dieth,
  For friends are round his bed,
And many a young lip sigheth
  When they name the early dead:
But weep for him that liveth
  Where none will know or care,
When the groan his faint heart giveth
  Is the last sigh of despair.

Weep not for him that dieth,
  For his struggling soul is free,
And the world from which it flieth
  Is a world of misery;
But weep for him that weareth
  The captive's galling chain:
To the agony *he* beareth,
  Death were but little pain.

Weep not for him that dieth,
  For he hath ceased from tears,
And a voice to his replieth
  Which he hath not heard for years;
But weep for him who weepeth
  On that cold land's cruel shore—
Blest, blest is he that sleepeth,—
  Weep for the dead no more!

THE CHILD OF EARTH.

FAINTER her slow step falls from day to day,
  Death's hand is heavy on her darkening brow•
Yet doth she fondly cling to earth, and say,
  "I am content to die, but, oh! not now!
Not while the blossoms of the joyous spring
  Make the warm air such luxury to breathe;
Not while the birds such lays of gladness sing·
  Not while bright flowers around my footsteps wreathe.

Spare me, great God, lift up my drooping brow!
I am content to die—but, oh! not now!"

The spring hath ripen'd into summer-time,
The season's viewless boundary is past;
The glorious sun hath reach'd his burning prime;
Oh! must this glimpse of beauty be the last?
'Let me not perish while o'er land and lea,
With silent steps the lord of light moves on;
Nor while the murmur of the mountain bee
Greets my dull ear with music in its tone!
Pale sickness dims my eye, and clouds my brow;
I am content to die—but, oh! not now!"

Summer is gone, and autumn's soberer hues
Tint the ripe fruits, and gild the waving corn;
The huntsman swift the flying game pursues,
Shouts the halloo, and winds his eager horn.
"Spare me awhile to wander forth and gaze
On the broad meadows and the quiet stream,
To watch in silence while the evening rays
Slant thro' the fading trees with ruddy gleam!
Cooler the breezes play around my brow;
I am content to die—but, oh! not now!"

The bleak wind whistles, snow-showers, far and near,
Drift without echo to the whitening ground;
Autumn hath pass'd away, and, cold and drear,
Winter stalks on, with frozen mantle bound.

Yet still that prayer ascends:—"Oh! laughingly
My little brothers round the warm hearth crowd,
Our home-fire blazes broad, and bright, and high,
And the roof rings with voices glad and loud;
Spare me awhile! raise up my drooping brow!
I am content to die—but, oh! not now!"

The spring is come again—the joyful spring!
Again the banks with clustering flowers are spread;
The wild bird dips upon its wanton wing:—
The child of earth is number'd with the dead!
"Thee never more the sunshine shall awake,
Beaming all readily thro' the lattice-pane;
The steps of friends thy slumbers may not break,
Nor fond familiar voice arouse again!
Death's silent shadow veils thy darken'd brow;
Why didst thou linger?—thou art happier now!"

THE CHRISTENING.

Helpless thou liest, thy little waxen face
Eagerly scann'd by our inquiring glances,
Hoping some lovely likeness there to trace,
Which fancy finds and so thy worth enhances;

Clothing with thought mature, and power of
mind,
Those infant features, yet so faintly lined.

And still thy youthful mother bendeth down
Her large, soft, loving eyes, brimful of gladness,
Her cheek almost as waxen as thine own,
Her heart as innocently free from sadness:
And still a brighter smile her red lip wears,
As each her young son's loveliness declares.

And sometimes as we gaze a sigh is heard,
(Though from the happy group all grief seems
banish'd')
As thou recallest, little nestling bird,
Some long familiar face whose light hath
vanish'd;
Some name, which yet hath power our hearts to
thrill—
Some smile whose buried beauty haunts us still!

Ah! most to Her, the early widow'd, come
Thoughts of the blossoms that from earth
have perish'd;
Lost to her lone and solitary home,
Though in her brooding memory fondly
cherish'd:—
Her little grandson's baby smiles recall
Not *one* regretted hope of youth, but *all!*

Her Son's son lies upon her cradling knee,
And bids her heart return, with mournful dreaming,
To her own first born's helpless infancy,
When hope—youth's guiding star—was brightly beaming;
And He, who died too soon, stood by and smiled,
And bless'd alike the mother and her child.

Since then, how many a year hath fleeted past!
What unforseen events, what joys, what sorrows,
With sunshine or with clouds have overcast
The long succession of her lonely morrows;
Ere musing o'er this fair and new-born face,
A fresh link carried on her orphan'd race!

Fair child, that race is not by man's award
Ennobled,—but by God; no titles sounded
By herald's trump, or smooth and flattering bard,
Proclaim within what lines *thy* rank is bounded:—
Thy power hereditary none confine,
The gift of Genius, boy, by right is thine!

Be humble, for it is an envied thing;
And men whose creeping hearts have long submitted
Around the column'd height to clasp and cling
Of Titled Pride—by man to man transmitted,—

Will grudge the power they have less cause to
dread,
Oppose the living, and malign when dead.

One of thy lineage served his country well
(Though with her need her gratitude departed;)
What in her memory now is left to dwell?
The *faults* of him who died half broken-heart-
ed:—
And those, whose envious hands ne'er stretch'd
to save,
Pluck down the laurels springing from his grave.

Yet hush! it is a solemn hour; and far
Be human bitterness and vain upbraiding;
With hope we watch thy rising, thou young star,
Hope not *all* earthly, or it were too fading;
For we are met to usher in thy life,
With prayer,—which lifteth hearts, and quell-
eth strife!

Hush'd is the busy group, and still as death;
All at the sacred altar meekly kneeling;
For *thy* sake, who so lately drew thy breath,
All unto Heaven with earnest heart appealing.
A solemn voice addresses the Most High,
And with a murmuring echo we reply.

All holy be the hour! and, oh! may Heaven
Look down and bless the anxious mother's
part,
As meekly she confides the treasure given

So lately to her young and hoping heart;
And pleads that God's great love may be his stay,
And guide her little Wanderer on his way.

So let it be! and when the noble head
Of thy true-hearted father, babe beloved,
Now glossy dark, is silver-gray instead,
And thy young birth-day far away removed;
Still may'st thou be a comfort and a joy,—
Still welcome as this day, unconscious boy!

THE MOTHER'S LAST WATCH.

Written on the occasion of the death of the infant daughter of Her Grace the Duchess of Sutherland.

Hark, through the proudly decorated halls,
How strangely sounds the voice of bitter woe,
Where steps that dread their echo as it falls
Steal silently and sadly to and fro.
There wither'd lies the bud so lately given,
And, beautiful in grief as when she smiled,
Bow'd 'neath the unexpected stroke of Heaven,
The mourning Mother watches o'er her Child.

Tis her last Watch! Sleep seals those infant lids

Dark fall the lashes on that roseleaf cheek—
But oh!—the look is there, which Hope forbids;
Of Death—of Death those heavy eyelids speak!—
'Tis her last Watch!—no more that gentle hand
With cautious love shall curtain out the light—
No more that graceful form shall mutely stand
And bless thy slumbers thro' the shadowy night.

Hush'd is the innocent heart which throbbing pain,
Vain hope, and vain regret had never moved.
The God who gave hath claim'd his gift again,
And angels welcome her, on earth so loved.
Yet still of hope and fear the endless strife
Within that Mother's bosom faintly swells,
Still, still she gazes on, and dreams of life,
Though the fond falsehood Reason's pow'r repels.

Unheard each word of comfort faintly falls
From lips whose tones in other days were dear,
Her infant's smile is all her heart recalls,—
Her infant's voice is all her heart can hear;—
She clasps its hand, the feverish glow of *hers*
Wakes into warmth the freezing current's flow;
She bends,—her sobbing breath a ringlet stirs
With mimic life upon its pallid brow.

Oh! what a mournful thing is human love!
In happier days of hope and bliss gone by,
The Mother's heart with pitying throb would move
If but a tear drop dimm'd that laughing eye:
And now she prays that Heaven the boon may give
To hear from those pale lips a cry of pain—
Aught that could bid her sinking soul revive,
And tell the mourner thou wert *hers* again!

Ah! never more that dream of hope may be!—
The summer breeze among the boughs shall wave,
The summer sun beam bright o'er land and lea,
But thou, no spring shall wake thee from the grave!
No more those little rosy lips shall greet
With brightly sudden smile her look of pride;
No more with falt'ring steps those fairy feet
Shall totter onward to her cherish'd side.

All, all is over! See, with painful start
She wakens from her trance to feel the whole,
And know the pang even from thy *corse* to part—
Thou vainly guarded treasure of her soul!
The hand that, ah! so often hath caress'd,
Aids now to place thee in thy narrow bed!
The last wild kiss upon thy cheek is press'd—
The last fond tear upon thy coffin shed!
And all is hush'd: but oft thro' Life's dull track
(When time her present sorrow hath beguiled)

That pale, sweet brow shall dimly bring us back
The Mother's last Watch o'er her fairy Child!

THE ARAB'S FAREWELL TO HIS HORSE.

My beautiful! my beautiful!
That standest meekly by
With thy proudly arched and glossy neck,
And dark and fiery eye;
Fret not to roam the desert now,
With all thy winged speed—
I may not mount on thee again—
Thou'rt sold, my Arab steed!
Fret not with that impatient hoof—
Snuff not the breezy wind—
The further that thou fliest now,
So far am I behind;
The stranger hath thy bridle rein—
Thy master hath *his* gold—
Fleet-limbed and beautiful! farewell!—
Thou'rt sold, my steed—thou'rt sold!

Farewell! those free untired limbs
Full many a mile must roam,
To reach the chill and wintry sky,
Which clouds the stranger's home;
Some other hand, less fond, must now

Thy corn and bread prepare:
The silky mane I braided once,
Must be another's care!
The morning sun shall dawn again,
But never more with thee
Shall I gallop through the desert paths,
Where we were wont to be:
Evening shall darken on the earth;
And o'er the sandy plain
Some other steed, with slower step,
Shall bear me home again.

Yes, thou must go! the wild, free breeze,
The brilliant sun and sky,
Thy master's home—from all of these,
My exiled one must fly.
Thy proud, dark eye will grow less proud,
Thy step become less fleet.
And vainly shalt thou arch thy neck,
Thy master's hand to meet.
Only in sleep shall I behold
That dark eye, glancing bright—
Only in sleep shall hear again
That step so firm and light:
And when I raise my dreaming arm
To check or cheer thy speed,
Then must I starting wake, to feel—
Thou'rt *sold*, my Arab steed!

Ah! rudely then, unseen by me,
Some cruel hand may chide.

Till foam-wreaths lie, like crested waves
  Along thy panting side:
And the rich blood that's in thee swells,
  In thy indignant pain,
Till careless eyes, which rest on thee,
  May count each started vein.
Will they ill use thee? If I thought–
  But no, it cannot be—
Thou art so swift, yet easy curbed;
  So gentle, yet so free.
And yet, if haply when thou'rt gone,
  My lonely heart should yearn—
Can the hand which casts thee from it now
  Command thee to return?

Return!—alas! my Arab steed!
  What shall thy master do,
When thou who wert his all of joy,
  Hast vanished from his view?
When the dim distance cheats mine eye,
  And through the gathering tears
Thy bright form, for a moment,
  Like the false mirage appears.
Slow and unmounted will I roam,
  With weary foot alone,
Where with fleet step, and joyous bound,
  Thou oft has borne me on;
And sitting down by that green well,
  I'll pause and sadly think,
"It was here he bowed his glossy neck,
  When last I saw him drink!"

When last I saw thee drink !—away !
  The fevered dream is o'er—
I could not live a day, and *know*
  That we should meet no more!
They tempted me, my beautiful!
  For hunger's power is strong—
They tempted me my beautiful!
  But I have loved too long.
Who said that I had given thee up ?—
  Who said that thou wert sold ?
'Tis false,—'tis false, my Arab steed !
  I fling them back their gold!
Thus, *thus*, I leap upon thy back,
  And scour the distant plains ;
Away ! who overtakes us now,
  Shall claim *thee* for his pains.

THE FEVER-DREAM.

It was a fever-dream ; I lay
Awake, as in the broad bright day,
But faint and worn I drew my breath
Like those who wait for coming death ;
And my hand lay helpless on my pillow
Weak as a reed or bending willow ;
And the night-lamp, with its shadowy veil,
And its light so sickly, faint, and pale ;
Gleamed mournfully on objects round;

And the clock's stroke was the only sound ;
Measuring the hours of silent time
With a heavy and unwelcome chime,
As still monotonously true
To its pulse-like beat, the minutes flew.

I was alone, but not asleep ;
Too weary, and too weak to weep,
My eyes had closed in sadness there ;
And they who watched o'er my despair
Had placed that dim light in the room,
And deepened the surrounding gloom,
By curtaining out the few sad rays
Which made things present to my gaze ;
And all because they vainly thought
At last the night its rest had brought,—
Alas ! rest came no more to me
So heavy was my misery !

They left me, and my heart was filled
With wandering dreams, whose fancies thrilled
Painfully through my feeble brain,
Till I almost wished them back again.
Yet wherefore should I bid them stay ?
They could not chase those dreams away,
But only watch me as I lay.

They left me, and the midnight stroke
From the old clock the silence broke,
And with a wild repining sigh
I wished it were my time to die !

And then, with spirit all dismayed,
For that wild wish, forgiveness prayed,
Humbling myself to God's high power
To bear His will, and wait His hour.

And while I darkly rested there,
The breath of a young child's floating hair,
Perfumed, and warm, and glistening bright,
Swept past me in the shrouding night;—
And the footsteps of children, light and quick,
(While my heart beat loud, and my breath came
thick)
Went to and fro on the silent floor;—
And the lock was turned in the fastened door,
As a child may turn it, who tiptoe stands
With his fair round arms and his dimpled hands,
Putting out all their strength in vain
Admittance by his own means to gain:
Till his sweet impatient voice is heard
Like the chirp of a young imprisoned bird,
Seeking an entrance still to win
By fond petitions to those within.

A child's soft shadowy hair, bright smiles,
His merry laugh, and coaxing wiles,
These are sweet things,—most precious things,—
But in spite of my brain's wild wanderings,
I knew that they dwelt in my fancy only,
And that I was sad, and left, and lonely;
And the fear of a dreadful madness came
And withered my soul like a parching flame;
And I felt the strong delirun growing,

And the thread of my feeble senses going,
And I heard with a horror all untold
Which turned my hot blood icy-cold,
Those light steps draw more near my bed;
And by visions I was visited,
Of the gentle eyes which I might not see,
And the faces that were so far from me!

And blest, oh! blest was the morning beam
Which woke me up from my fever-dream!

ATARAXIA.

Come o'er the green hills to the sunny sea!—
The boundless sea that washeth many lands,
Where shells unknown to England, fair and free,
Lie brightly scattered on the gleaming sands.
There, 'midst the hush of slumbering ocean's roar,
We'll sit and watch the silver-tissued waves
Creep languidly along the basking shore,
And kiss thy gentle feet, like Eastern slaves.

And we will take some volume of our choice,
Full of a quiet poetry of thought;
And thou shalt read me, with thy plaintive voice,

Lines which some gifted mind hath sweetly wrought.
And I will listen, gazing on thy face—
Pale as some cameo on th' Italian shell—
Or looking out across the far blue space
Where glancing sails to gentle breezes swell.

Come forth! The sun hath flung on Thetis' breast
The glittering tresses of his golden hair;
All things are heavy with a noonday rest,
And floating sea-birds leave the stirless air.
Against the sky, in outlines clear and rude,
The cleft rocks stand, while sunbeams slant between;
And lulling winds are murmuring through the wood
Which skirts the bright bay with its fringe of green.

Come forth! All motion is so gentle now,
It seems *thy* step alone should walk the earth—
Thy voice alone, the 'ever soft and low,
Wake the far-haunting echoes into birth.
Too wild would be Love's passionate store of hope—
Unmeet the influence of his changeful power;
Ours be Companionship, whose gentle scope
Hath charm enough for such a tranquil hour.

In *that*, no jealously—no wild regret
Lies like deep poison in a flower's bright cup,

Which thirsty lips for ever seek, and yet
For ever murmur as they drink it up.
The memory of *thy* beauty ne'er can rise
With haunting bitterness in days to come;
Thy name can never choke my heart with sighs,
Nor leave the vex'd tongue faltering, faint, and dumb.

Therefore come forth, oh gentle friend! and roam
Where the high cliffs shall give us ample shade,
And see how glassy lie the waves, whose foam
Hath power to make the seaman's heart afraid.
Seek thou no veil to shroud thy soft brown hair—
Wrap thou no mantle round thy graceful form;
The cloudless sky smiles forth as still and fair
As though earth ne'er could know another storm.

Come! Let not listless sadness make delay—
Beneath Heaven's light that sadness will depart;
And as we wander on our shoreward way,
A strange, sweet peace shall enter in thine heart.
We will not weep, nor talk of vanish'd years,
When, link by link Hope's glittering chain was riven;

Those who are dead shall claim from love no tears—
  Those who have injured us shall be forgiven.

Few have my summers been, and fewer thine;
  Youth ruined, is the weary lot of both;
To both, all lonely shows our life's decline—
  Both with old friends and ties have waxed wroth.
But yet we will not weep! The breathless calm
  Which lulls the golden earth, and wide blue sea,
Shall pour into our souls mysterious balm,
  And fill us with its own tranquillity.

We will not mar the scene—we will not look
  To the veil'd future, or the shadowy past;
Seal'd up shall be sad Memory's open book,
  And Childhood's idleness return at last!
Joy, with his restless, ever-fluttering wings,
  And Hope, his gentle brother—all shall cease;
Like weary hinds that seek the desert springs,
  Our one sole feeling shall be peace—deep peace!

Then come! Come o'er the green hills to the sea—
  The boundless sea that washeth many lands
And with thy plaintive voice, oh! read to me,
  As we two sit upon the golden sands.

And I will listen, gazing on that face—
  Pale as some cameo on th' Italian shell—
Or looking out across the far blue space
  Where glancing sails to gentle breezes swell!

ON SEEING ANTHONY ASHLEY.

Ah! then, what dreams of proud success,
  That lordly brow of beauty brought,
With all its infant stateliness,
  And all its unripe power of thought!
What triumphs, boundless, unconfined,
Came crowding on my wand'ring mind.

I gave that child, the voice might hold
  A future senate in command;
Head clear and prompt—heart true and bold
  As quick to act as understand:
I dream'd the scholar's fame achieved—
The hero's wreath of laurel weaved!

But as I mused, a whisper came
  Which (like a friend's reproachful tone,
Whose gentleness can smite with shame
  Far more than fiercest word or frown;)
Roused my vex'd conscience by its spell,
And thus the whisper'd warning fell:—

"Ah! let the shrouded future be,
  With all its weight of distant care'

Cloud not with dreams of vanity,
That blue bright eye, and forehead fair!
Nor cast *thy* worldly hopes and fears
In shadow o'er his happy years!

"Desire not, even in thy dreams,
To hasten those remoter hours
Which, bright although their promise seems,
Must strip his spring-time of its flowers!—
What triumph, in the time to come,
Shall match these early days of *home?*

"*This* is the Eden of his life,—
His little heart bounds glad and free:
Amid a world of toil and strife,
All independent smileth he!
Nor dreams by that sweet mother's side
Of dark Ambition's restless pride.

'But, like a bird in winter,—still
Fill'd with a sweet and natural joy,
Tho' frost lies bleak upon the hill,
And mists obscure the cold grey sky,
Which sings, tho' on a leafless bough,—
He smiles, even at the gloomiest brow!"

Oh! looking on a child's fair face
Methinks should purify the heart;
As angel presences have grace
To bid the darker powers depart,
And glorify our grosser sense
With a reflected innocence!

And seeing thee, thou lovely boy,
My soul, reproach'd, gave up its schemes
Of worldly triumph's heartless joy,
For purer and more sinless dreams,
And mingled in my farewell there
Something of *blessing* and of *prayer.*

THE CHAPEL ROYAL ST. JAMES'S.

And they come forth anew,
In bridal white, that gentle virgin band,
The chosen flowers of Britain's happy land:
For holy love and true
Hath wrought an hour of hope without alloy—
A fairy sight of splendour and of joy.

There,—with her locks of light,
Gleaming like gold around her noble head,—
The orphan'd Eleanor, with stately tread,
Went by, a vision bright;
Bidding sweet thoughts of love and triumph start
Into a father's and a sister's heart.

There,—in her beauty, pass'd
Young Frances Cowper her transparent cheek
Blushing the greetings which she might not speak,
As on the crowd she cast

The shy soft glances of those soft blue eyes,
In whose unfathom'd depth such sweetness lies!

There, with her spotless name,
The gentle HOWARD, good, and fair, and mild,
And bright eyed BOUVERIE, noble Radnor's child,
And rose-bud VILLIERS came;
And, with her sweet frank smile, young IDA HAY,
Looking all gladness, like a morn in May.

There, brilliant LENNOX moved;
The Paget beauty shining from her brow,
And the dark, deer-like eyes that glanced below:
While, gentle and beloved,
Amid the glories of that courtly throng,
DELAWARR's youthful daughter pass'd along.

There, (theme for poet's praise!)
With swanlike throat, and clear majestic eye,
VERULAM's stately MARY glided by;—
And, with her quiet gaze
Fix'd smiling on the scene which she survey'd,
The soldier ANGLESEA's bright ADELAIDE.

And she, whose orbs of blue,
Like mountain lakes beheld by moonlight, gleam
With all the shadowy softness of a dream
Such as Endymion knew

Whose glossy locks with rich luxuriance twine
Around her brow: the Lady WILHELMINE.

Young were they all—and fair,—
But thou, VICTORIA, held'st thy fitting place,
As amongst garden-flowers the lily's grace,
Blooms with a royal air;
And from that lovely various group, apart,
Did'st stand, and gently look the queen thou art.

The smile thy young lip wore,
Spoke joy to Him, who, from his distant home,
Hath sped in wintry time o'er ocean's foam—
To seek our island shore,
With his frank heart, and brow so fair and true,
Claiming thy love—and England's welcome too.

Oh! may that welcome prove
The herald of deep gladness;—since in thee
Old England's brightest hopes renew'd we see
All-hallow'd be thy love;
And still with proud content the day allied,
When Princely ALBERT claim'd his Royal Bride!

May He, whose gifted hand,
Hath twined sweet wreaths of Poetry and Song
Live happy among English hearts so long
That, native to the land,
He shall forget that e'er his harp was strung,
To any accents but our mother-tongue:

And thou,—Oh! may the Crown
Which in youth's freshest, earliest moment graced
The brow, whose childhood's roses it replaced,
Ne'er weigh thy spirits down;
Nor tearful hours, nor careful thoughts, beguile
One ray of gladness from thy gracious smile:

But brightly to the last,
Fair fortune shine, with calm and steady ray,
Upon the tenor of thy happy way;
A future like the past:
And every prayer by loyal subjects said,
Bring down a separate blessing on thy head!

BY CHIDICK TYCHBORN,

BEING YOUNG, AND THEN IN THE TOWER, THE NIGHT BEFORE HIS EXECUTION.

My prime of youth is but a frost of cares,
My feast of joy is but a dish of pain,
My crop of corn is but a field of tares,
And all my good is but vain hope of gain,
The day is past, and yet I saw no sun;
And now I live, and now my life is done!

The spring is past, and yet it hath not sprung,
The fruit is dead, and yet the leaves are green,

My youth is gone, and yet I am but young,
I saw the world, and yet I was not seen,
My thread is cut, and yet it is not spun;
And now I live, and now my life is done!

I sought my death, and found it in my room,
I look'd for life, and saw it was a shade,
I trod the earth, and knew it was my tomb,
And now I die, and now I am but made:
The glass is full, and now my glass is run;
And now I live, and now my life is done!

SPRING.

The Spring is come! the breath of May
Creeps whisperingly where brightest flowers have birth,
And the young sun peeps forth with redder ray
On the broad bosom of the teeming earth.
The Spring is come! how gladly nature wakes
From the dark slumber of the vanished year
How gladly every gushing streamlet breaks
The summer stillness with its music clear!

But thou art old, my heart! the breath of Spring
No longer swells thee with a rapturous glow
The wild bird carols blithely on the way,

But wakes no smile upon my withered brow.
Thou art grown old! no more the generous thought
Sends the warm blood more swiftly through the veins—
Selfish and cold thou shrinkest—Spring hath nought
For *thee* but memory of vanished pains.

The day-break brings no bounding from my rest,
Eagerly glad, and strong in soul and limb;
But through the weary lid (unwelcome guest!)
The sunlight struggles with a lustre dim.
The evening brings no calm—the night no sleep,
But feverish tossings on the hateful bed;
While the vexed thoughts their anxious vigils keep,
Yet more to weary out the aching head.

Still the deep grove—the bower—my footsteps seek:
Still do I read beneath the flowery thorn;
And with a worn and hollow-eaten cheek,
Woo the young freshness of the laughing morn.
But now no pleasure in the well-known lines
Expands my brow, or sparkles in mine eye;
O'er the dull page my languid head declines,
And wakes the echo with a listless sigh.

Ah! mocking wind, that wandereth o'er my form,
With freshened scents from every opening flower;
Deep—deep within the never-dying worm—
Life's longing's all unquenched, defy the power!
There coolness comes not with the cooling breeze—
There music flows not with the gushing rill—
There shadows calm not from the spreading trees—
Unslaked, the eternal fever burneth still!

Mock us not, Nature, with thy symbol vain
Of hope succeeding hope, through endless years—
Earth's buds may bu'st—earth's groves be green again,
But man—can man forget youth's bitter tears?
I thirst—I thirst! but duller day by day
Grow the clogg'd soarings of my spirit's wing;
Faintly the sap of life slow ebbs away,
And the worn heart denies a second Spring.

THE FAITHFUL GUARDIAN.*

Small need of care! The stately hound, still calm and couchant lies,
With lazy kindness lifting up his wise and honest eyes;
Declaring by the emblem meet of his serene repose,
How frankly generous hearts can bear the baiting of mean foes.

Not so, O! noble-natured brute, would'st thou quiescent rest,
If the sound of danger roused the blood within thy valiant breast;
If near these helpless little fays,—thy master's children—came
The doubtful tread of stranger's feet, on whom they had on claim;

Then, *then*, upspringing with a bound,—aroused for their defence,—

* Suggested by Mr. Edwin Landseer's celebrated Picture of the Marquis of Abercorn's Children.

Each nerve would arm with savage strength thy keen and eager sense,
And the darkly gleaming eyes where now such softened shadows play,
Would burn like watch-fires, lit at night, to scare the foe away.

And were the danger *real* to these, by whom thy watch is kept,—
E'er a rough hand should dare profane the cradle where they slept,
E'er a rude step should reach the spot where now they smile at play,—
Thy fangs would meet within his throat, to hold the wretch at bay!

Thou would'st battle, noble creature, for these children of thy lord's,
As *men* fight for a Royal Prince, whose crown hangs on their swords;—
Soldiers, who hear their General's cry by treachery hemm'd in,—
Freeman, who strike for home and earth, 'gainst Tyranny's proud sin,—
So would'st thou strive! And bold were he who then could lay thee low,
For still thy fierce and mighty grasp would pin the struggling foe,
And if keen sword, or human skill cut short thy gasping breath,
Should *he* be thought thy conqueror?—No!—
Thy conqueror would be Death.

Oh, tried and trusted! Thou whose love ne'er
changes nor forsakes,
Thou proof how perfect God hath stamped the
meanest thing he makes;
Thou, whom no snare entraps to serve, no art
is used to tame,—
(Train'd, like ourselves, thy path to know, by
words of love and blame;)
Friend! who beside the cottage door, or in the
rich man's hall,
With steadfast faith still answerest the one
familiar call,—
Well by poor hearth and lordly home thy couch-
ant form may rest,
And Prince and Peasant trust thee still, to
guard what they love best!

XARIFA.

One eve at spring-tide's close we took our way,
When eve's last beams in soften'd glory fell,
Lighting her faded form with sadden'd ray,
And the sweet spot where we so lov'd to
dwell.
Faintly and droopingly she sat her down
By the blue waters of the Guadalquiver,
With darkness on her brow, but yet no frown,
Like the deep shadow on that silent river.
She sat her down, I say, with face upturn'd

To the dim sky, which daylight was forsak
ing,
And in her eyes a light unearthly burn'd—
The light which spirits give whose chains are
breaking!

And a half smile lit up that pallid brow,
As, casting flowers upon the silent stream,
She watch'd the frail, sweet blossoms glide and
go
Like human pleasure in a blissful dream.
And then with playful voice she gently flung
Small shinning pebbles from the river's brink,
And o'er the eddying waters sadly hung,
Pleased, and yet sorrowful, to see them sink.
"And thus," she said, "doth human love for
get
Its idols--some sweet blessings float away,
Follow'd by one long look of vain regret,
As they are slowly hastening to decay;

And some, with sullen plunge, do mock our
sight,
And suddenly go down into the tomb,
Startling the beating heart whose fond delight
Chills into tears at that unlook'd for doom.
And there remains no trace of them save such
As the soft ripple leaves upon the wave,
Or a forgotten flower, whose dewy touch
Reminds us some are withering in the grave
When all is over, and she is but dust,
Whose heart so long hath held thy form en
shrined:

When I go hence, as soon as feel I must,
  Oh! let my memory, Isbal, haunt thy mind.
When in thy daily musing thou dost bring
  Those scenes to mind in which I had a share;
When in thy nightly watch thy heart doth wring
  With thought of me—Oh! murmur forth a prayer!
A prayer for me—for thee—for all who live
  Together, yet asunder, in one home—
Who their soul's gloomy secret dare not give,
  Lest it should blacken all their year to come.
Yes, Isbal, yes; to *thee* I owe the shade
  That prematurely darkens on my brow;
And never had my lips a murmur made—
  But—but that—see! the vision haunts me now!"
She pointed to the river's surface, where
  Our forms were pictured seated side by side;
I gazed on them and hers was very fair;
  And mine—was as thou seest it *now*, my bride.
But hers, though fair, was fading—wan and pale
  The brow whose marble met the parting day,
Time o'er her form had thrown his misty veil,
  And all her ebon curls were streak'd with grey;
But mine was youthful—yes!—such youth as glows
  In the young tree by lightning scathed and blasted—
That, joyless, waves its black and leafless boughs,
  On which spring showers and summer warmth are wasted.

THE FLIGHT OF XERXES.

I SAW him on the battle eve,
  When like a king he bore him!
Proud hosts in glittering helm and greave,
  And prouder chiefs before him:
The warrior, and the warrior's deeds,
The morrow, and the morrow's meeds,—
  No daunting thoughts came o'er him;—
He look'd around him, and his eye
Defiance flash'd to earth and sky!

He look'd on ocean,—its broad breast
  Was covered with his fleet;
On earth,—and saw from east to west
  His banner'd millions meet:
While rock, and glen, and cave, and coast,
Shook with the war-cry of that host,
  The thunder of their feet!
He heard the imperial echoes ring—
He heard, and *felt* himself a king!

I saw him next alone;—nor camp
  Nor chief his steps attended,

Nor banners' blaze nor coursers' tramp,
  With war-cries proudly blended :—
He stood alone, whom Fortune high
So lately seem'd to deify,
  He who with heaven contended
Fled, like a fugitive and slave ;
Behind, the foe,—before, the wave !

He stood,—fleet, army, treasure gone,
  Alone, and in despair !
While wave and wind swept ruthless on,
  For *they* were monarchs there ;
And XERXES in a single bark,
Where late his thousand ships were dark,
  Must all thy fury dare ;—
Thy glorious revenge was this,
Thy trophy, deathless SALAMIS !

—♦—

THE CARELESS WORD.

A WORD is ringing thro' my brain,
It was not meant to give me pain ;
It had no tone to bid it stay,
When other things had passed away
It had no meaning more than all
Which in an idle hour fall :
It was when *first* the sound I heard
A lightly uttered, careless word.

That word—oh! it doth haunt me now,
In scenes of joy, in scenes of woe;
By night, by day, in sun or shade,
With the half smile that gently played
Reproachfully, and gave the sound
Eternal power thro' life to wound.
There is no voice I ever heard,
So deeply fix'd as that one word.

When in the laughing crowd some tone,
Like those whose joyous sound is gone,
Strikes on my ear, I shrink—for then
The careless word comes back again.
When all alone I sit and gaze
Upon the cheerful home-fire blaze,
Lo! freshly as when first 'twas heard,
Returns that lightly uttered word.

When dreams bring back the days of old,
With all that wishes could not hold;
And from my feverish couch I start
To press a shadow to my heart—
Amid its beating echoes, clear
That little word I seem to hear:
In vain I say, while it is heard,
Why weep?—'twas but a foolish word.

It comes—and with it come the tears,
The hopes, the joys of former years;
Forgotten smiles, forgotten looks,
Thick as dead leaves on autumn brooks,

And all as joyless, though they *were*
The brightest things life's spring could share.
Oh! would to God I ne'er had heard
That lightly uttered, careless word!

It was the first, the only one
Of these which lips forever gone
Breathed in their love—which had for me
Rebuke of harshness at my glee:
And if those lips were heard to say,
"Beloved, let it pass away,"
Ah! then, perchance—but I have heard
The last dear tone—the careless word!

Oh! ye who, meeting, sigh to part,
Whose words are treasures to some heart,
Deal gently, ere the dark days come,
When earth hath but for *one* a home;
Lest, musing o'er the past, like me,
They feel their hearts wrung bitterly,
And, heeding not what else they heard,
Dwell weeping on a careless word.

THEY LOVED ONE ANOTHER.

They loved one another! young Edward and his wife,
And in their cottage-home they dwelt, apart from sin and strife.

Each evening Edward weary came from a day
of honest toil,
And Mary made the fire blaze, and smiled a
cheerful smile.
Oh! what was wealth or pomp to them, the
gaudy glittering show,
Of jewels blazing on the breast, where heaves
a heart of woe!
The merry laugh, the placid sleep, were theirs
they hated sloth,
And all the little that they had, belonged alike
to both,
For they loved another!

They loved one another; but one of them is
gone,
And by that vainly cheerful hearth poor Edward
sits alone.
He gazes round on all which used to make his
heart rejoice,
And he misses Mary's gentle smile, he misses
Mary's voice.
There are many in this chilly world who would
not care to part,
Tho' they dwell together in one home, and
ought to have one heart,
And yet *they* live! while never more those hap-
py ones may meet;
And the echo from her home is gone, of Mary's
busy feet:
And *they* loved one another!

They loved one another! but she hath passed away,
And taken with her all the light, the sunshine of his day;
And Edward makes no loud lament, nor idly sits and mourns,
But quietly goes forth at morn, and quietly returns.
The cottage now is still and dark, no welcome bids him home,
He passes it and wanders on, to sit by Mary's tomb.
Oh! weep my friends—for very sad and bitter it must be
To yearn for some familiar face we never more may see—
When we loved one another!

MY CHILDHOOD'S HOME.

I HAVE tasted each varied pleasure,
And drunk of the cup of delight;
I have danced to the gayest measure
In the halls of dazzling light.
I have dwelt in a blaze of splendour,
And stood in the courts of kings;
I have snatched at each toy that could render

More rapid the flight of Time's wings.
But vainly I've sought for joy or peace,
In that life of light and shade;
And I turn with a sigh to my own dear home—
The home where my childhood played!

When jewels are sparkling round me,
And dazzling with their rays,
I weep for the ties that bound me
In life's first early days.
I sigh for one of the sunny hours
Ere day was turned to-night;
For one of my nosegays of fresh wild flowers,
Instead of those jewels bright.
I weep when I gaze on the scentless buds
Which never can bloom or fade;
And I turn with a sigh to those gay green fields—
The home where my childhood played.

OLD FRIENDS.

How are they waned and faded from our hearts,
The old companions of our early days!
Of all the many loved, which name imparts
Regret when blamed, or rapture at its praise?
What are their several fates, by Heaven decreed,

They of the jocund heart, and careless brow?
Alas! we scarcely know and scarcely heed,
Where, in this world of sighs, they wander now.

See, how with cold faint smile, and courtly nod,
They pass, whom wealth and revelry divide—
Who walked together to the house of God,
Read from one book, and rested side by side;
No look of recognition lights the eye
Which laughingly hath met that fellow face;
With careless hands they greet and wander by,
Who parted once with tears and long embrace.

Oh, childhood! blessed time of hope and love,
When all we knew was Nature's simple law,
How may we yearn again that time to prove,
When we looked round, and loved what'er we saw.
Now dark suspicion wakes, and love departs,
And cold distrust its well-feigned smile displays;
And they are waned and faded from our hearts,
The old companions of our early days!

WHEN POOR IN ALL BUT HOPE AND LOVE.

When, poor in all but hope and love,
I clasped thee to my faithful heart;
For wealth and fame I vowed to rove,
That we might meet no more to part!
Years have gone by—long weary years
Of toil, to win thee comfort now—
Of ardent hopes—of sickening fears—
And wealth is mine—but where art *thou?*

Fame's dazzling dreams, for thy dear sake,
Those brighter than before to me;
I clung to all I deemed could make
My burning heart more worthy thee.
Years have gone by—the laurel droops
In mockery o'er my joyless brow:
A conquered world before me stoops,
And Fame is mine—but where art *thou?*

In life's first hours, despised and lone,
I wandered through the busy crowd;
But now that life's best hopes are gone,

They greet with pride and murmurs loud.
Oh! for thy voice! thy happy voice,
To breathe its laughing welcome now;
Wealth, fame, and all that should rejoice,
To me are vain—for where art *thou*?

WE HAVE BEEN FRIENDS TOGETHER.

We have been friends together,
In sunshine and in shade;
Since first beneath the chesnut trees
In infancy we played.
But coldness dwells within thy heart,
A cloud is on thy brow;
We have been friends together—
Shall a light word part us now?

We have been gay together;
We have laughed at little jests;
For the fount of hope was gushing
Warm and joyous in our breasts.
But laughter now hath fled thy lip,
And sullen glooms thy brow;
We have been gay together—
Shall a light word part us now?

We have been sad together,
We have wept with bitter tears,

O'er the grass-grown graves, where slumbered
The hopes of early years.
The voices which are silent there
Would bid thee clear thy brow;
We have been *sad* together—
Oh! What shall part us now?

THE MOURNERS.

Low she lies, who blest our eyes
  Through many a sunny day;
She may not smile she will not rise—
  The life hath past away!
Yet there is a world of light beyond,
  Where we neither die nor sleep—
She is *there*, of whom our souls were fond—
  Then wherefore do we weep?

The heart is cold, whose thoughts were told
  In each glance of her glad bright eye;
And she lies pale, who was so bright,
  She scarce seemed made to die.
Yet we know that her soul is happy now,
  Where the saints their calm watch keep;
That angels are crowning that fair young brow—
  Then wherefore do we weep?

Her laughing voice made all rejoice,
  Who caught the happy sound;

There was gladness in her very step,
  As it lightly touched the ground.
The echoes of voice and step are gone;
  There is silence still and deep:
Yet we know she sings by God's bright throne—
  Then wherefore do we weep?

The cheek's pale tinge, the lid's dark fringe,
  That lies like a shadow there,
Were beautiful in the eyes of all—
  And her glossy golden hair!
But though that lid may never wake
  From its dark and dreamless sleep,
She is gone were young hearts do not break·
  Then wherefore do we weep?

That world of light with joy is bright,
  This is a world of woe:
Shall we grieve that her soul hath taken flight,
  Because we dwell below?
We will bury her under the mossy sod,
  And one long bright tress we'll keep;
We have only given her back to God—
  Ah! wherefore do we weep?

WOULD I WERE WITH THEE!

WOULD I were with thee! every day and hour
Which now I spend so sadly, far from thee—
Would that my form possessed the magic power
To follow where my heavy heart would be!
Whate'er thy lot—by land or sea—
Would I were with thee—eternally!

Would I were with thee! when, the world forgetting,
Thy weary limbs upon the turf are thrown,—
While bright and red the evening sun is setting,
And all thy thoughts belong to heaven alone:
While happy dreams thy heart employ—
Would I were with thee—in thy joy!

Would I were with thee! when, no longer feigning
The hurried laugh that stifles back a sigh!
Thy young lip pours unheard its sweet complaining,
And tears have quenched the light within thine eye:

When all seems dark and sad below,
Would I were with thee—in thy woe!

Would I were with thee! when the day is breaking,
And when the moon hath lit the lonely sea—
Or when in crowds some careless note awaking:
Speaks to thy heart in memory of me.
In joy or pain, by sea or shore—
Would I were with thee—evermore!

THE CAPTIVE PIRATE.

The captive pirate sat alone,
Musing over triumphs gone,
Gazing on the clear blue sky
From his dungeon window high.
Dreamingly he sate, and thought
Of battles he had seen and fought;
And fancy o'er him threw her spell.
He deemed he had not bid farewell
To the friends who loved him best:
O'er the white wave's snowy crest
Seems he now once more to sail,
Borne by the triumphant gale:
Cheerily the light bark bounds.
In his ears the music sounds
Of hoarsely mingled waves and voices,

And his inmost soul rejoices!
He gives the signal of command,
He waves—he drops—the lifted hand!
It was a sound of clashing steel—
Why starts he thus? what doth he feel?
The clanking of his iron chain
Hath made him prisoner *again!*
He groans, as memory round him brings
The shades of half-forgotten things.
His friends! his faithful friends!—a sigh
Bursts from that bosom swelling high.
His bark! his gallant bark!—a tear
Darkens the eye that knew not fear.
And another meaner name
Must lead *his* men to death or fame!
And another form must stand
(Captain of his mourning band)
On the deck he trod so well,
While his bark o'er ocean's swell
Is sailing far, far out at sea,
Where he never more may be!
Oh! to be away once more
From the dark and loathsome shore!
Oh! again the sound to hear
Of his ship's crew's hearty cheer!
Souls who by his side have stood,
Careless of their ebbing blood,
Wiped the death-dew from their brow,
And feebly smiled their truth to show.
Little does the Pirate deem
Freedom now were but a dream;
Little does the chieftain think

That his lost companions drink
Strugglingly by the salt sea wave,
Once their home, and now their grave!
And the bark from which they part,
(While his sad and heavy heart
Yearns to tread her gallant deck,)
Helpless lies, a heaving wreck!—

And little will *they* deem, who roam
Hereafter in their floating home,
While their sunlit sail is spread,
That it gleams above the dead--
That the faithless wave rolls on
Calmly, as they were not gone,
While its depths warm hearts doth cover
Whose beatings were untimely over!
And little will they deem, who stand
Safe upon the sea-girt land,
'That to the stranger all it gave
Was--a prison and a grave!
That the ruin'd fortress towers
Number'd his despairing hours,
And beneath their careless tread,
Sleeps--the broken-hearted dead!

THE FUTURE.

I WAS a laughing child, and gaily dwelt
Where murmuring brooks, and dark blue rivers
roll'd,
And shadowy trees outspread their silent arms,
To welcome all the weary to their rest.
And there an antique castle raised its head,
Where dwelt a fair and fairy girl: perchance
Two summers she had seen beyond my years;
And all she said or did, was said and done
With such a light and airy sportiveness,
That oft I envied her, for I was poor.
And lowly, and to me her fate did seem
Fraught with a certainty of happiness.
Years past; and she was wed against her will,
To one who sought her for the gold she brought,
And they did vex and wound her gentle spirit,
Till madness took the place of misery.
And oft I heard her low, soft, gentle song,
Breathing of early times with mournful sound,
Till I could weep to hear, and thought how
sad,
The envied *future* of her life had prov'd.

And then I grew a fond and thoughtful girl,
Loving, and deeming I was lov'd again:
But he that won my easy heart, full soon
Turn'd to another:—she might be more fair,
But could not love him better. And I wept,
Day after day, till weary grew my spirit,
With fancying how happy she must be
Whom he had chosen—yet she was not so;
For he she wedded, loved her for a time,
And then he changed, even as he did to me,
Though something later; and he sought another
To please his fancy, far away from home.
And he was kind: oh, yes! he still was kind.
It vexed her more; for though she *knew* his love
Had faded like the primrose after spring,
Yet there was nothing which she might complain,
Had cause to grieve her; he was gentle still.
She would have given all the store she had,
That he would but be angry for an hour,
That she might come and sooth his wounded spirit,
And lay her weeping head upon his bosom,
And say, how freely she forgave her wrongs:
But still, with calm, cold kindness he pursued
(Kindness, the mockery of departed love!)
His way—and then she died, the broken hearted;
And I thanked heaven, who gave me not her lot,

Though I had wish'd it.
Again, I was a wife, a happy wife;
And he I loved was still unchangeable,
And kind, and true, and loved me from his soul;
But I was childless, and my lonely heart
Yearned for an image of my heart's beloved,
A something which should be my 'future' *now*
That I had so much of my life gone by;
Something to look to after I should go,
And all except my memory be past.
There was a child, a little rosy thing,
With sunny eyes, and curled and shining hair,
That used to play among the daisy flowers,
Looking as innocent and fair as they;
And sail its little boat upon the stream,
Gazing with dark blue eyes in the blue waters,
And singing in its merriment of heart
All the bright day: and when the sun was setting,
It came unbid to its glad mother's side,
To lisp with holy look its evening prayer:
And, kneeling on the green and flowery ground,
At the sweet cottage door—he fixed his eyes
For some short moments on her tranquil face,
As if *she* was his guiding star to God;
And then with young, meek, innocent brow upraised,
Spoke the slow words with lips that longed to smile,
But dared not. Oh! I loved, that child with all
A mother's fondest love; and, as he grew

More and more beautiful from day to day,
The half-involuntary sigh I gave
Spoke but too plain the wish that he were mine—
My child—my own. And in my solitude,
Often I clasped my hands and thought of him,
And looked with mournful and reproachful gaze
To heaven, which had denied me such a one.
Years past: the child became a rebel boy;
The boy a wild, untamed, and passionate youth;
The youth a man—but such a man! so fierce,
So wild, so headlong, and so haughty too,
So cruel in avenging any wrongs,
So merciless when he had half avenged them!
At length his hour had come—a deed of blood,
Of *murder*, was upon his guilty soul.
He stood in that same spot, by his sweet home,
The same blue river flowing by his feet,
(Whose stream might never wash his guilt away;)
The same green hills, and mossy sloping banks,
Where the bright sun was smiling as of yore:
With pallid cheek and dark and sullen brow,
The beautiful and lost; you might have deemed
That Satan, newly banished, stood and gazed
On the bright scenery of an infant world.
For, fallen as he was, his Maker's hand
Had stamped him beauteous, and he was so *still*.
And his eyes turned from off his early home
With something like a shudder; and they lighted

On his poor broken-hearted mother's grave.
And there was something in them of old times,
Ere sin had darkened o'er their tranquil blue,
In that most mournful look—that made me weep;
"For I had gazed on him with fear and anguish
Till now. And, 'weep for *her*,' my favourite said,
For she was good—I murdered her—I killed
Many that harmed me not." And still he spoke
In a low, listless voice; and forms came round
Who dragged him from us. I remember not
What followed then. But on another day
There was a crowd collected, and a cart
Slowly approached to give to shameful death
Its burden; and there was a prayer, and silence,
Silence like that of death. And then a murmur!
And all was over. And I groaned, and turned
To where his poor old father had been sitting;
And there he sate, still with his feeble limbs
And palsied head, and dim and watery eyes,
Gazing up at the place where was his *son;*
And with a shuddering touch I sought to rouse him,
But could not for the poor old man was dead.
And then I flung myself upon the ground,
And mingled salt tears with the evening dew;
And thanked my God that he was *not* my son
And that I was a childless, lonely wife.
To-morrow I will tell thee all that now

Remains to tell—but I am old and feeble,
And cannot speak for tears.

She rose and went,
But she returned no more. The morrow came,
But not to her;—the tale of life was finished,
Not by her lips, for she had ceased to breathe.
But, by *this* silent warning joined to hers,
How little we may count upon the future,
Or reckon what that future may bring forth.

THE RINGLET.

Oh! treasured thus by passion's slave,
Dear relic of the bygone year;
Say, what remains of her who gave?
The vain regret—the useless tear.
The clasping hands—the throbbing brow—
The murmuring of that shadowy word,
To which had answered once—oh! now,
Why is that light quick step unheard?

What in those syllables is found,
That such a start of woe can claim?
A word is but an empty sound,—
Alas! it is—it *was*—her name!
It was—yes, *she* was once! as gay,
As full of life, as aught that lives;

The breath—the life--hath passed away
  But not the pang her memory gives.

Bright tress thy beauty bringeth now
  A thousand dreams of rapture gone;
Her sunny eyes, her radiant brow,
  The low, light laughter of her tone.
Gazing on thee, again she stands
  Before me, as in days of old;
With all her young head's shining bands,
  And all its wavy curls of gold.

Till as I view thee, silken tress,
  I feel within my suffering heart,—
'Tis all which now my sight can bless,
  All that of *her* will not depart.
Oh! thou that wert life's dearest prize,
  That now art but a thought of pain;
Why do thy tones—thy laughing eyes
  Rise up to wring my soul again?

I roam in vain: the sun that beams
  Is still the sun *we* looked upon;
My hand, my lonely hand, in dreams,
  Seeks still for thine to clasp its own.
My heart resists all time—all change,
  And finds no other form so dear.
My memory, wheresoe'er I range,
  Clings to the spot where *thou* wert near.
Change! *thou* wert all life's scenery:
  To me, the billowy, bounding wave—
The wide green earth—the far blue sky,
  Form but the landscape of thy grave!

Oh! bitter is their boon of life
  Who cannot hope—who may not die—
I linger in a world of strife,
  Whilst *thou* art in the happy sky!
I envy thee the peace thou hast,
  And, but 'tis sin, the knee would bow,
That He who made thee all thou *wast*,
  Would make *me* all—that thou art now!

THE HEART'S WRECK

The lulling winds may still the sea,
  All beautiful in its repose;
And with a soft tranquility
  The rippling water ebbs and flows.

But when the tempests wildly blow,
  Its bosom heaves with many a wreck
Which, till that moment, slept below,
  Nor dimmed its surface with a speck.

So *I* can talk, and laugh, and seem
  All that the happiest souls could be;
Lulled for a moment, by some dream,
  Soft as the sunset on the sea.

But when a word, a tone, reminds
  My bosom of its perished love,

Oh! fearful are the stormy winds
Which dash the *heart's* wild wrecks above!

One after one they rise again,
And o'er dark memory's ocean steal,
Floating along, through years of pain—
Such as the heart-struck only feel!

THE LOST ONE.

Come to the grave--the silent grave! and dream
Of a light, happy voice—so full of joy,
That those who heard *her* laugh, would laugh again,
Echoing the mirth of such an innocent spirit;
And pause in their own converse, to look round,
Won by the witchery of that gleesome tone.
Come to the grave—the lone dark grave! and dream
Of eyes whose brilliancy was of the soul,
Eyes which, with one bright flash from their dark lids,
Seemed at a glance to read the thoughts of others;
Or, with a full entire tenderness,
The pure expression of all-perfect love,
(Of woman's love, which is for you alone,
While your's is for yourself)—gave in that look

The promise of a *life* of meek affection.
Come to the grave—the mouldering grave! and dream
Of a fair form that glided over earth
One of its happiest creatures:—to her cheek
The lightest word might bring the blushing blood
In pure carnation;—down her graceful neck,
The long rich curls of jet hung carelessly,
Untortured by the cunning hand of art:
And on her brow, bright purity and joy,
Twin sisters, sate,—as on a holy throne.
Come yet unto the grave—the still, damp grave!
And dream of a young heart that beat with life,
And all life's best affections; of a heart
Where sorrow never came, nor fear, nor sin—
Nor aught save innocence, and perfect love:
And, having dreamed of such a lovely being—
So gay, so bright, so pure, so fond, so meek—
Having thus conjured up a form of love
In thine own pausing and regretful mind;
A vision will be present to thy soul,
A faint, but faithful portraiture, of one
Most dearly loved, and now for ever lost!

MY NATIVE LAND.

FROM THE GERMAN OF KORNER.

WHERE is the minstrel's native land?
Where the flames of light and feeling glow;
Where the flowers are wreathed for beauty's brow;
Where the bounding heart swells strong and high,
With holy hopes which may not die—
There is my native land!

What is that bright land's music name?
Ere it bent its neck to a foreign yoke,
It was called the land of the broad strong oak—
The land of the free—the German land—
But her sons lie slain by the stranger's hand,
And she weeps sad tears of shame.

Why does the minstrel's country weep?
That the hurricane's rage hath bowed the pride
Of those who should stem the rising tide;
That her princes quail—and that none will hear
Her holy words of might and fear—
Therefore my land must weep!

To whom does the minstrel's country call?
It calls to the silent heavenly powers,
With despair, as the thunder darkly lowers,
For its freedom—for those who should break its chain—
For the hand that never strikes in vain—
To *these* doth my country call!

For what does the minstrel's country sigh?
That the bloodhound may hunt beyond the bound
Of the soil which brave hearts make holy ground;
That the serf may cease; and our sons be free,
Or those who have borne them, cease to be—
For this does my country sigh!

And still doth the minstrel's country hope?
Her hope is firm, for her cause is good—
That her brave will rise, and her true in blood;
And that God the avenger, our fathers' God,
Will mark the tears that bedew her sod—
Such is my country's hope!

DREAMS.

Surely I heard a voice—surely my name
Was breathed in tones familiar to my heart!
I listened--and the low wind stealing came,
In darkness and in silence to depart.

Surely I saw a form, a proud bright form,
Standing beside my couch! I raised mine eyes:
'Twas but a dim cloud, herald of a storm,
That floated through the grey and twilight skies.

Surely the brightness of the summer hour
Hath suddenly burst upon the circling gloom!
I dream; 'twas but the perfume of a flower,
Which the breeze wafted through the silent
room.

Surely a hand clasped mine with greetings fond!
A name is murmured by my lips with pain;
Woe for that sound—woe for love's broken
bond.
I start—I wake—I am alone again!

RECOLLECTIONS.

Do you remember all the sunny places,
Where in bright days, long past, we played together?
Do you remember all the old home faces
That gathered round the hearth in wintry weather?
Do you remember all the happy meetings,
In Summer evenings round the open door—
Kind looks, kind hearts, kind words and tender greetings,
And clasping hands whose pulses beat no more?
Do you remember them?

Do you remember all the merry laughter;
The voices round the swing in our old garden:
The dog that, when we ran, still followed after;
The teazing frolic sure of speedy pardon:
We were but children *then*, young happy creatures,
And hardly knew how much we had to lose—
But *now* the dreamlike memory of those features
Comes back, and bids my darkened spirit muse.
Do you remember them?

Do you remember when we first departed
From all the old companions who were round us,
How very soon again we grew light-hearted,
And talked with smiles of all the links which bound us?
And after, when our footsteps were returning,
With unfelt weariness, o'er hill and plain;
How our young hearts kept boiling up, and burning,
To think how soon we'd be at home again,
Do you remember this?

Do you remember how the dreams of glory
Kept fading from us like a fairy treasure;
How we thought less of being famed in story,
And more of those to whom our fame gave pleasure.
Do you remember in far countries, weeping,
When a light breeze, a flower, hath brought to mind,
Old happy thoughts, which till that hour were sleeping,
And made us yearn for those we left behind?
Do you remember this?

Do you remember when no sound 'woke gladly,
But desolate echoes through our home were ringing,
How for a while we talked—then paused full sadly,
Because our voices bitter thoughts were bringing?

Ah me! those days—those days! my friend,
my brother,
Sit down and let us talk of all our woe,
For we have nothing left but one another;—
Yet where *they* went, old playmate, *we* shall go—
Let us remember this.

THE GREEK GIRL'S LAMENT FOR HER LOVER.

IMRA! thy form is vanished
From the proud and patriot band;
Imra! thy voice is silent,
'Mongst the voices of the land.
And bravely hast thou fallen!
In joy didst thou depart;
Their chains shall never bind thee,
Young hero of my heart!

But with *thee* the dream is over
That bound my soul so long;
And the words of fame and glory
Have vanished from my song:
My heart which bounded proudly
Is as sad as sad can be;
I thought it beat for freedom,
But I feel it beat—*for thee.*

I thought the victory's triumph
Would have made my soul rejoice,
But that was when I listened
To the music of thy voice.
The dreams of fame and conquest,
Of my country being free;
What love were they to Zoo,
But most blessed dreams of *thee?*

It is past—thy voice may never
Speak of triumph, or of love;
And the bright hope that was burning
Hath flown with thee above.
This earth contains no dwelling,
No land of rest for me;
When Hellas *was* my country,
I dwelt in it with *thee!*

MARY.

Yes, we were happy once, and care
My jocund heart could ne'er surprise;
My treasures were, her golden hair,
Her ruby lips, her brilliant eyes.
My treasures were—alas! depart
Ye visions of what used to be!
Cursed be the heart—the cruel heart—
That stole my Mary's love from me.

Dark are my joyless days—and thou—
  Dost *thou* too dream, and dreaming weep?
Or, careless of thy broken vow,
  Unholy revels dost thou keep?
No, Mary, no,—we loved too well,
  Such deep oblivion cannot be;
Cursed be the lips, where guile could dwell,
  To lure thy love away from me!

It cannot be!—ah! haply, while
  With wild reproach I greet thy name,
Thy ruby lip hath ceased to smile—
  Thy happy head is bowed with shame!
Haply, with haggard want opprest,
  Thou weepest where no eye may see;
  Cursed be the spoiler's cruel breast—
  But, oh! my Mary!—heaven shield *thee!*

THE PILGRIM OF LIFE.

PILGRIM, who toilest up life's weary steep,
  To reach the summit still with pleasure crowned;
Born but to sigh and smile; to sin and weep,
  Dost mark the busy multitudes around?
Dost mourn, with those who tread with fainting feet,
  And blighted worn-out heart, the self same road?

Dost laugh with those who think their travel
 sweet,
 And deem existence no unwelcome load ?—
Ah, no! unconscious of *their* joy or woe,
 Quick hurrying onward still, or gazing back,
With feeble lustre round their planet glow
 A few beloved, connected with thy track;
Dear links of life, for whom to toil is bliss;
 Circlet of stars in young hope's diadem;
Gay lightsome hearts who know no joy but
 this—
 To be *together* is enough for them.
Thou pausest on thy way—one light is set—
No power of love relumes the torch of life;
Whate'er it was, 'tis lost—and vain regret
Pursues the rosy babe, or faithful wife.
'Tis past—'tis gone—the brightness of those eyes
Can cheer no more thy melancholy home:
But grief may not endure—new joys arise;
The past is not—but thou hast years to come!
New joys arise—eager thou pressest on,
Hope's brilliant mockery deceiving still.
And now thou weepest o'er delusions gone,
Now hail'st with transport days devoid of ill.
Yet ever as thou goest on thy way,
However bright may be the present hour,
Clings to thy mind with brighest, purest ray,
The joy thou could'st not hold, the faded flow-
 er—
Still dearest seems the *past*; and as each light,
Extinguished, leaves thee lone, through mem
 ory's tears

More dim the *future* rises to thy sight,
More bright the visions of thine early years.
Pilgrim of Life! why slackenest thou thy speed!
Why is that brow of eager hope o'ercast?
A pause—a struggle—and the hour decreed
Mingles for aye the *present* with the *past*!

TO A BLIND CHILD.

Thou wreck of human hopes! whose darkened eyes
No more behold the blue and sunny skies,
Doomed in thy joyous childhood's early day
Blindly to grope along thy cheerless way;
Ere yet the bitter tear of sorrow streaming
Had clouded those sweet orbs, or dimmed their beaming,
It was foretold that fate—and now, alas!
The awful prophecy hath come to pass.
Oh, thou unhappy! in thy infant hours
How glad thy parents watch'd thy dawning powers;
O'er thy young innocence enraptured hung,
Praised the soft murm'ring accents of thy tongue,
And guessed thy meaning, not from *words* alone,

But from the speaking orbs that brightly shone—
That glorious feature of the human face,
That silent language nothing can replace.
They watched, as slowly stealing, ray by ray,
That gentle light was fading fast away;
And wept, in sad and hopeless agony,
O'er the dimmed glance of thy half-conscious
eye.
At length it ceased, and darkness then dwelt
there,
Unbroken—cheerless—deep as their despair!
Mournful, expressionless, they turn to those
Who watched with rapture once their lids un-
close;
And from those darkened orbs is slowly steal-
ing
The only trace *now* left of earthly feeling,
A tear—a silent tear, condemned to flow
For vanished joys or years of future woe.
Oh! far more moving is that look to *me*
Than all the supplicating agony—
The pearly drops that fall from Beauty's eyes,
Her bursting sobs, her low and melting sighs.
Mourners there be of whom we soothe the pain,
And, where we pity, pity not in vain;
But here there is a look which seems to say,
Thou canst do nought for me—we turn away
Sick at the heart. O thou lamented one!
Perchance long years are thine to spend alone!
No gladsome child shall frolic by thy side,
Thy feeble age some stranger hand shall guide
Or faithful dog, with dumb, imploring glance,

Collect the half-reluctant alms:—perchance,
Wandering and-weary, thou shalt lay thy head
In the poor shelter of some ruined shed;
Or rest thy worn-out form beneath a tree,
While darken o'er thee skies thou canst not see—
While dreadful night the trembling world enshrouds,
And the hoarse thunder struggles through the clouds,
Then, while the bitter blast is howling round,
Defenceless *thou* shalt stretch thee on the ground;
And cowering by his helpless master's side,
Like thee forsaken, and all help denied,
The sole companion of thy cheerless track
Shake the cold rain-drops from his shivering back,
And shrinking, shuddering, of the storm afraid,
Seek aid from thee—*thou* canst not give him aid.
In such an hour, perchance, thou'lt breathe thy last,
Thy dirge the moaning of the wintry blast!
Shield, shield his houseless head, all-pitying Heaven!
When far in eddying rounds the snow is driven!
Whom *man* neglects, stretch *thou* thy hand to save,
Protect the transient life thy mercy gave;

Let him not die, nor leave *one* friend behind
To echo those sad words—"Pity the poor old blind!"

MARRIAGE AND LOVE.

THE poorest peasant of the meanest soil,
The child of poverty, and heir to toil,
Early, from radiant love's impartial light,
Steals one small spark to cheer his world of night:
Dear spark! which oft, through winter's chilling woes,
Is all the warmth his little cottage knows!

SHERIDAN.

LAURA was lightsome, gay, and free from guile;
Bright were her eyes, and beautiful her smile;
Women found fault, but men were heard to swear
That she *was* lovely, though she was not *fair.*
Her parents were not rich, nor very poor;
She had enough, nor breathed a wish for more;
Blithe were the mornings, gay the evenings spent,
And youthful eyes smiled back a calm content.
Yes, she was happy, and she was at rest,
Till the world filled with cares her little breast

Taught her to fear all dowagers and mothers,
Smile on gay lords, and cut their younger brothers.
This last rule cost her now and then a sigh—
'Tis wrong to say so—but I know not why
Men, when they're handsome, are not liked the less,
And may be pleasant, though they're penny-less—
But Laura's mother never would agree
That needy men could pleasant partners be ;
To gain *her* favour, vain was all exertion,
A younger brother was her great aversion.
The mother hoped and prayed—her prayer was granted,
A lordling came—the very thing she wanted—
"Oh ! what a match, my dear !"—and Laura sighed
And hung her head, and timidly replied,
"She did not love,"—'What put it in your head
That it was needful ?—you are asked to *wed*—
Romantic love is all a childish folly,
So marry, dear ! and don't look melancholy ;
Besides, you cannot always live at home—
Another year your sister's turn will come—
And you will be *so* rich !—where *shall* we go ?
Let us begin to think of your *trousseau* !"
And Laura laughed, and looked up at her mother :
She loved not *him*—but then, she loved no other !
Days passed away—she spent the last few hours

In pinning on lace veils and orange flowers;
With beating heart the maid to church was carried,
And Laura blushed, and trembled, and—was married!
Quickly the happy couple sped away,
And friends' congratulations end the day.
"Sweet girl! how well she look'd! dress'd with such care!
How the rich veil became her face and hair!
A lovely woman, certainly,"—and Laura
Left friends behind, with all the world before her!
Dwelt for a while (remembrance sad and strong!)
In Laura's mind her little brother's song—
The quick light step—the blue and sparkling eye,
The bright perfection of his infancy—
Her sister's gentle smile—all these arise,
Whilst damp'd her wedding veil her weeping eyes;
But soon consoled, again the maid grew gay,
Swift in amusement flew each busy day;
The country seat was exquisite; she found
New beauties every time she looked around;
The lawn so green, so smooth, so sunny too,
The flowers so bright, the heavens of *such* a blue!—
"Oh! this *was* happiness!"—It *might* have been
Had there been no reverse of this fair scene.

But Laura's lord was not what lords should be;—
Cold, harsh, unfeeling, proud, alas! was he—
And yet a *very* fool—had he been stern,
She would have tried the tyrant's will to learn—
Had he been passionate, she still had loved—
Or jealous, time her virtue would have proved;
But, as he was, without a soul or mind,
Too savage e'en to be in seeming kind—
The slave of petty feelings, every hour
He changed his will, to show he *had* the power;
And Laura wept, that she had linked her fate
With one too cold to love, too mean to hate.
A mother's hopes were left her, and she said,
'My child, at least, will love me!' days, months, sped—
She watched the grave, and wept the early dead!
The scene was changed: nought pleases Laura now,
Nor sunny sky, nor richly sweeping bough;
At the long window, opening to the ground,
She sits, while evening spreads its shadows round;
Or through the glowing noon, for weary hours,
Watches the bees that flutter o'er the flowers;
Or when the moon is up, and stars are out
She leaves her lonely room to roam about,
And while the night breeze murmurs o'er her head,
Upbraids the living, or bewails the dead!
Both are alike insensible—her mate,
Weary of home, hath left her to her fate;

Nor recks he *now* that Laura weeps or sighs,
So he enjoy what Heaven to *her* denies.
But there was *one* who thought eyes blue and deep,
Like Laura's were too beautiful to weep;
Perchance he told her so—perchance she guessed
He deemed her lovelier than his words expressed—
A cousin he of Laura's moody lord,
But how unlike him!—every gentle word
And gentlier tone—the song, the walk, the book,
The graceful step, the bright expressive look,
Awoke in her a deep and sad regret
Of what he *might* have been—ah! might be yet!
And yet she struggled with her yielding heart—
'Twas sin to meet—but oh! 'twas grief to part!
He never *said* he loved her—could she cry,
"Francis! you love me; Francis; you must fly?"
Perchance he loved her not—Alas! too well
Each knew the passion neither dared to tell.
Mute would they stand, upon some summer eve,
With melancholy rapture, prone to grieve;
Then, trembling, gaze upon each other's eyes,
The heaven of each, more worshipped than the skies.
Her lord returned—he saw her flushing cheek,
Her vain attempt to smile, or freely speak;
"Thou hast been false! I'll know the truth,"
He cried in fury—"Who's the favour'd youth?

Wretch! I will tear the minion limb from
limb!"
But Laura's heart was full, her eye was dim:
She answered not, with faint, slow step withdrew,
Of Francis thought—and then to Francis flew.
"Thou knowest—God knows!"—no more the
maiden said,
But on his shoulders dropped her sobbing head;
And Francis, as his arm was cast around her
(The first wild moment that fond arm e'er
bound her),
Murmured,—"My love! my life! what, if we
flee?
The world!—the world!—what is that world to
me?
Thou art *my* world—I, thine—" and her reply
Was but a stifled sound—half sob, half sigh.

* * * * *

Oh! it is wretched, when the loss of fame
Hath left us but the shadow of a name—
When all forget us, all refuse to own,
And life is journey'd on, alone—*alone*!
'Tis bitter then to see the flame of love,
The only link for which we still would prove
Life's withering joys, expiring spark by spark,
Till *all* extinct, and we left lone and dark!
Thus Francis' love consumed itself away,
While mournful Laura drooped from day to
day—
Her graceful Francis, all his passion o'er,
Grieved she had fallen to rise again no more—

Grieved that harsh scorn should hail her blighted name,
Grieved that she had felt and saw *he* felt her shame.
At length he shunned her, and poor Laura sighed,
Murmured repentant prayers to Heaven—and died.
And then no more her Francis blamed the wife
Who left her mate to lead a guilty life;
No more he feels, what fond proud hearts *must* feel,
Who blush for those whose wounds they cannot heal,
But turned with fond regret, and useless call,
To her who with him had abandoned all!

* * * * *

* * * * *

And Francis, loved again, is happy now;
For he hath chosen him a gentle bride.
With gay light heart, and pure and placid brow
Unused to grief, and impotent to chide.
But hapless Laura, where is *she* the while?
The light gay form is mouldering in the grave;
The full and rosy lip hath ceased to smile,
And all is gone which bounteous Nature gave;

Pulseless the heart, and spiritless the eye,
Whence flashed a soul for better feelings framed;
The eloquent tongue with dust is choked and dry:
She sinned—she wept—and is no more ashamed.

THE WANDERER LOOKING INTO OTHER HOMES.

A LONE, wayfaring wretch I saw, who stood
  Wearily pausing by the wicket gate;
And from his eyes there streamed a bitter flood
  Contrasting *his* with many a happier fate.
Bleak howled the wind, the sleety shower fell
    fast
  On his bare head, and scanty-covered breast;
As through the village with quick step I past,
  To find sweet shelter in my home of rest.

"Oh! that I too could call a home my own!"
  Said the lone wanderer, as he wistful gazed
Through the clear lattice, on the hearth's wide
    stone,
  Where cheerily the jocund fire blazed.
"Oh! that I too, in such a cot might dwell!
  Where the bright homefire blazeth clear and
    high:
Where joy alone my grateful heart might swell,
  And children's children bless me when I
    die!"

Little he deemed what bitterness was there,
  Who murmured thus his aspirations vain,—
Little he deemed that one as fond as fair
  Lay faintly sighing on a bed of pain:
And by her side, a restless vigil keeping,
  One who had deeply wronged that gentle heart—
Knelt with clasped hands; now praying, and now weeping;
  Dreading, each hour, to see the soul depart.

They were two sisters jealous love had twained;
  And one had slandered her who faded lay,
Because she deemed her slighted love disdained:
  And he they both had loved was far away:
And from that hour, the younger drooped and pined,
  Like a pale snowdrop bowing down her head;
Joyless of life—to slow disease resigned—
  The heart within her was already dead.

Here, for her sake, they woo the mountain gale,
  If, haply, change may yet prevent her fate.
But he, the wanderer, knew not of this tale,
  And humbly sues admittance at their gate.
He enters, what hath met his eager eyes?
  Pale as the white-fringed drapery spread beneath,
His early loved, his sorely slandered, lies,

Heaving with pain her faint and quickened
breath.

O'er her soft arm her long, dark, glossy hair
Floats in unbraided beauty,—and her cheek,—
Ah, me! the deeply-crimsoned tinge is there,
That of sharp woe and early death doth
speak.
How beautiful, beneath her drooping eye,
The glowing hectic of that cheek appears,
Where the long lashes like soft shadows lie,
Seeking in vain to prison back her tears.

She gazes—shrieks—'tis he! at length '*tis* he,
Whom dreams and waking thoughts have
brought in vain!
And must she die, e'er yet from sorrow free,
Her head hath rested on his heart again?
A few slow, bitter words of wild appeal—
Of earnest explanation faintly given—
A pressure, which his hand can scarcely feel,
And her freed soul is on its way to heaven.

So, wanderers in the world may pausing gaze
Upon some radiant form with smiles of light,
And seeing but the outward beam that plays,
Envy their joys—and deem that all is bright.
The homes of other hearts! oh! yet beware,
Ye, who with friendly guise would enter in.

Lest all be false,—and ye be doomed to share
Their guilt or woe—their sadnees or their sin!

MUSIC'S POWER.

HAVE you never heard, in music's sound,
Some chords which o'er your heart
First fling a moment's magic round,
Then silently depart?
But with the echo on the air,
Roused by that simple lay,
It leaves a world of feeling there
We cannot chase away.
Yes, yes,—a sound hath power to bid them come—
Youth's half-forgotten hopes, childhood's remembered home.

When sitting in your silent home
You gaze around and weep,
Or call to those who cannot come
Nor wake from dreamless sleep;
Those chords, as oft as you bemoan
"The distant and the dead,"
Bring dimly back the fancied tone

Of some sweet voice that's fled!
Yes, yes,—a sound hath power to bid them come—
Youth's half-forgotten hopes, childhood's remembered home.

And when, amid the festal throng,
You are, or would be gay—
And seek to while, with dance and song,
Your sadder thoughts away;
They strike those chords and smiles depart,
As, rushing o'er your soul,
The untold feelings of the heart
Awake, and spurn control!
Yes, yes,—a sound hath power to bid them come—
Youth's half-forgotten hopes, childhood's remembered home.

THE FAITHLESS KNIGHT.

The lady she sate in her bower alone,
And she gaz'd from the lattice window high,
Where a white steed's hoofs were ringing on,
With a beating heart, and a smother'd sigh.
Why doth she gaze thro' the sunset rays—
Why doth she watch that white steed's track—
While a quivering smile on her red lip plays?
'Tis her own dear knight—will he not look back?

The steed flew fast—and the rider past—
Nor paus'd he to gaze at the lady's bower;
The smile from her lip is gone at last—
There are tears on her cheek—like the dew on
a flower!
And "plague on these foolish tears," she said,
"Which have dimm'd the view of my young
love's track;
For oh! I am sure, while I bent my head,
It was then—it was *then* that my knight look'd
back."

On flew that steed with an arrow's speed;
He is gone—and the green boughs wave between:
And she sighs, as the sweet breeze sighs through
a reed,
As she watches the spot where he last has been.
Oh! many a sun shall rise and set,
And many an hour may she watch in vain
And many a tear shall that soft cheek wet,
Ere that steed and its rider return again!

FAREWELL.

FAREWELL! in tearless agony I part!
Beloved, the pang can cost thee little now;
The thought of triumph dwells within thy heart
The smile of triumph plays around thy brow.

But oh! when that is gone, when Time hath dimmed,
(If Time must *dim*) the glories of thine eye;
When the full cup of joy, which now is brimmed,
Drained by thine eager spirit, shall be dry;

When snows have mingled in the locks of youth,
And passion's power no more thy heart can warm;
Where the cold world shines forth in sorrow's truth,
And life itself is but a broken charm;

When the bright sun which gilds thy day is set,
A star's faint lustre may resume its reign;
I am contented that thou should'st forget—
All love thee *now*, but I will love thee *then*.

I WAS NOT FALSE TO THEE.

I WAS not false to *thee*, and yet
My cheek alone looked pale;
My weary eye was dim and wet,
My strength began to fail.
Thou wert the same; thy looks were gay,
Thy step was light and free;
And yet, with truth, my heart can say,
I was not false to *thee!*

I was not false to thee. yet now
Thou hast a cheerful eye,
With flushing cheek and drooping brow
I wander mournfully.
I hate to meet the gaze of men,
I weep where none can see;
Why do *I* only suffer, when
I was not false to *thee?*

I was not false to thee; yet oh!
How scornfully they smile,
Who see me droop, who guess my woe,
Yet court thee all the while.
'Tis strange! but when long years are past,
Thou wilt remember me;
Whilst I can feel until the last,
I was not false to *thee!*

OH! LIFE IS LIKE THE SUMMER RILL.

Oh! life is like the summer rill, where weary daylight dies;
We long for morn to rise again, and blush along the skies.
For dull and dark that stream appears, whose wat‹›rs, in the day.

All glad in conscious sunniness, went dancing on their way.
But when the glorious sun hath 'woke and looked upon the earth,
And over hill and dale there float the sounds of human mirth;
We sigh to see dav hath not brought its perfect light to all,
For with the sunshine on those waves, the silent shadows fall.
Oh! like that changeful summer rill, our years go gliding by,
Now bright with joy, now dark with tears, before youth's eager eye.
And thus we vainly pant for all the rich and golden glow,
Which young hope, like an early sun, upon its course can throw.
Soon o'er our half-illumined hearts the stealing shadows come,
And every thought that woke in light receives its share of gloom.
And we weep while joys and sorrows both are fading from our view,
To find, wherever sunbeams fall, the shadow cometh too!

THE NAME.

" What's in a name?"—SHAKSPEARE."

THY name was once the magic spell, by which
 my thoughts were bound,
And burning dreams of light and love were
 wakened by that sound ;
My heart beat quick when stranger tongues,
 with idle praise or blame,
Awoke its deepest thrill of life, to tremble at
 that name.

Long years—long years have passed away, and
 altered is thy brow ;
And we who met so gladly once, must meet as
 strangers now :
The friends of yore come round me still, but
 talk no more of thee ;
'Tis idle ev'n to wish it now—for what art *thou*
 to *me?*

Yet still thy name, thy blessed name, my lonely
bosom fills,
Like an echo that hath lost itself among the distant hills,
Which still, with melancholy note, keeps faintly
lingering on,
When the jocund sound that woke it first is
gone—for ever gone.

THE ONE YOU LOVED THE BEST.

Oh! love—love well, but only once! for never
shall the dream
Of youthful hope return again on life's dark rolling stream—
No love can match the early one which young
affection nurs'd;
Oh, no—the one you loved the best, is she you
loved the first.

Once lost—that gladsome vision past—a fairer
form may rise,
And eyes whose lustre mocks the light of starry
southern skies,
But vainly seek you to enshrine the charmer in
your breast,
For still the one you loved the first, is she you
loved the best.

Again—'tis gone—'tis past away—those gentle tones and looks
Have vanished like the feathery snow in summer's running brooks;
With weary pinions wandering love forsakes the heart, his nest,
And fain would rest again with her whom first you loved, and best.

Perchance some faithful one is found, when love's romance is o'er,
With her you safe through storms may glide, to reach life's farthest shore;
But all too cold and real now you deem your home of rest,
And you sigh for her you loved the first—for *her* you loved the *best.*

THE PURPLE AND WHITE CARNATION.

A FABLE.

T'was a bright May morn, and each opening flower
Lay sunning itself in Flora's bower;
Young Love, who was fluttering round, espied
The blossoms so gay in their painted pride;

And he gazed on the point of a feathered dart,
For mischief had filled the boy-god's heart;
And laughed as his bowstring of silk he drew,
And away that arrow at random flew:
Onward it sped like a ray of light,
And fell on a flower of virgin white,
Which glanced all snowy and pure at the sun,
And wept when his glorious course was run:
Two little drops on its pale leaves lay
Pure as pearls, but with diamond ray,
(Like the tear on Beauty's lid of snow,
Which waits but Compassion to bid it flow;)
It rested, that dart; and its pointed tip
Sank deep where the bees were wont to sip;
And the sickening flower gazed with grief
On the purple stains which dimmed each leaf,
And the crystal drops on its leaves that stood
Blushed with sorrow and shame till they turned
to blood.

t chanced that Flora, wandering by,
Beheld her flow'ret droop and die;
And Love laughed in scorn at the flower-queen's
woe,
As she vainly shook its leaves of snow.
Fled from her lip was the smile of light:—
"Oh! who hath worked thee this fell despite!
Thou who did'st harm, alas! to none,
But joyed'st all day in the beams of the sun!"
"'Twas Love!" said the flower, and a scented
sigh
Loaded the gale that murmured by.

'Twas Love! and the dew-drops that blushed
on the wound
Sank slow and sad to the pitying ground.

"'Twas Love!" said Flora: "accursed be the
power
That could blight the bloom of so fair a flower,
With whispers and smiles he wins Beauty's ears
But he leaves her nothing save grief and tears.
Ye gods! shall he bend with such tyranny still
The weak and the strong to his wanton will?
No! the hearts that he joins may rude discord
sever;
Accursed be his power for ever and ever."
She spoke, and wept; and the echo again
Repeated the curse, but all in vain—
The tyrant laughed as he fluttered away,
Spreading his rainbow wings to the day,
And settling at random his feathered darts
To spoil sweet flowers, or break fond hearts.

He fled—and the queen o'er her flower in vain
Poured the evening dew and the April rain,
The purple spots on her heart still were,
And she said, as she wept her fruitless care,
"The blight and the stain may be washed
away,
But what *Love* hath ruined must sink in decay."

O'er that sad lost flower she wails and grieves ;
And the drops that by mortals as dew are seen
Are the tears of the morning flower-queen.
And when men are gazing with fond delight
On its varied leaves, and call them bright,
And praise the velvet tints, and say
There never was flower more pure and gay
That flow'ret says, as it droops its head,
" Alas ! for the day when by love I bled ;
When my feathery flowers were pure and white
And my leaves had no earthly stain or blight,
When no chilling blasts around me blew,
And in Flora's garden of light I grew.
Oh ! the blight and the stain may be washed
away,
But what *Love* hath ruined must sink in decay."

THE BRIDE.

She is standing by her loved one's side,
A young and a fair and a gentle bride,
But mournfulness hath cross'd her face
Like shadows in a sunny place,
And wistfully her eye doth strain
Across the blue and distant main.
My home! my home!—I would I were
Again in joyous gladness there!

My home! my home!—I would I heard
The singing voice, like some small bird,
Of him, our mother's youngest child,
With light soft step, and features mild.—
I would I saw that dear one now,
With the proud eye and noble brow,
Whose very errors were more loved
Than all our reason most approved.
And she, my fairy sister, she,
Who was the soul of childish glee;
Who loved me so—oh, let me hear
Once more those tones familiar, dear,
Which haunt my rest; and I will smile
Even as I used to do erewhile.
I know that some have fall'n asleep—
I know that some have learnt to weep—
But my heart never feels the same
As when those light steps round me came
And sadness weighs my heavy eye
Beneath this cheerless stranger sky:
Tho' fewer now might round me come—
It is my home—my own old home!

She is back again in her sunny home,
And thick and fast the beatings come
Of that young heart, as round she sees
The same sweet flowers, the same old trees
But they, the living flowers she loved,
Are *they* the same? are *they* unmoved?—
No—time which withers leaf and stem
Hath thrown his withering change o'er them.
Where there was mirth, is silence now—

Where there was joy, a darkened brow—
The bounding step hath given place
To the slow stealing mournful pace;
The proud bright eye is now less proud,
By time and thought, and sickness bowed,
And the light singing voice no more
Its joyful carols echoes o'er,
But whispers; fearful some gay tone
May wake the thought of pleasures gone.
It *is* her home—but all in vain
Some lingering things unchanged remain:
The present wakes no smile—the past
Hath tears to bid its memory last.
She knew that some were gone—but oh!
She knew not—youth can never know
How furrowed o'er with silent thought
Are brows which grief and time have taught.
The murmuring of some shadowy word,
Which *was* a name—which now, unheard,
May wander thro' the clear cold sky,
Or wake the echo for reply:
The lingering pause in some bright spot
To dream of those who now are not:
The gaze that vainly seeks to trace
Lost feelings beaming on a face
Where time and sorrow, guiit and care,
Have past and left there withering there:—
These are her joys; and she doth roam
Around her dear but desert home;
Peopling the vacant seats, till tears arise,
And blot the dim sweet vision from her eyes.

FIRST LOVE.

Yes, I know that you once were my lover,
But that sort of thing has an end,
And though love and its transports are over,
You know you can still be—my *friend:*
I was young, too, and foolish, remember;
(Did you ever hear John Hardy sing?)
It was then, the fifteenth of November,
And this is the end of the Spring!

You complain that you are not well-treated
By my suddenly altering so;
Can I help it?—you're very conceited,
If you think yourself equal to Joe.
Don't kneel at my feet, I implore you;
Don't write on the drawings you bring;
Don't ask me to say, "I adore you,"
For, indeed, it is now no such thing.

I confess, when at Bognor we parted,
I swore that I worshipped you then—
That *I* was a maid broken-hearted,
And *you* the most charming of men.
I confess, when I read your first letter,

I blotted your name with a tear—
But, oh! I was young—knew no better,
Could I tell that I'd meet Hardy here?

How dull you are grown! how you worry,
Repeating my vows to be true—
If I said so, I told you a story,
For I love Hardy better than you!
Yes! my fond heart has fixed on another,
(I sigh so whenever he's *gone*,)
I shall always love you—as a *brother*.
But my heart is John Hardy's alone.

SONNETS.

SONNET I.

ON SEEING THE BUST OF THE YOUNG PRINCESS DE MONTFORT.

(In the studio of Bartolini, at Florence.)

SWEET marble! didst thou merely represent,
   In lieu of her on whom our glances rest,
Some common loveliness,—we were content,
   As with a modell'd beauty, well express'd;
But, by the very skill which makes thee seem
   So like HER bright and intellectual face,
The heart is led unsatisfied to dream;
   For sculpture cannot give the breathing grace,
The light which plays beneath that shadowy brow,
   Like sunshine on the fountains of the south,—
The blush which tints that cheek with roseate glow,—
   The smile which hovers round that angel-mouth:

No! such the form o'er which Pygmalion sigh'd--
Too fair to be complete while SOUL was still denied!

SONNET II.

RAPHAEL.

Bless'd wert thou, whom Death, and not Decay,
  Bore from the world on swift and shadowy wings,
Ere age or weakness dimm'd one brilliant ray
  Of thy rapt spirit's high imaginings!
While yet thy heart was full of fervid love,
  And thou wert haunted by resistless dreams
Of all in earth beneath, or Heaven above,
  On which the light ot beauty richest gleams,
Dead, but not deathlike, wert thou borne along,
  Silent and cold, oh thou that didst combine
Sculpture, and painting, and the gift of song;
  While on thy brow, and on that work divine*
Porn with thee, glow'd from thine Italian sky,
A light whose glory spoke of immortality!

* The celebrated picture of the Transfiguration (at which Raphael is said to have worked the evening before his death) was borne at the bier-head in the procession of his funeral.

SONNET III.

THE FORNARINA.

AND bless'd was she thou lovedst, for whose sake
Thy wit did veil in fanciful disguise
The answer which thou wert compell'd to make
To Rome's High Priest, and call'd her then "Thine Eyes;"*
Tho' of her life obscure there is no trace,
Save where its thread with THY bright history twines,—
Tho' all we know of her be that sweet face
Whose nameless beauty from thy canvass shines,—
Dependant still upon her Raphael's fame,
And but recorded by her low degree,
As one who had in life no higher claim
Than to be painted and be loved by thee;—
Yet would I be forgot, as she is now,
Once to have press'd my lips on that seraphic brow!

* Leo X., visiting Raphael in his studio, and seeing there the Fornarina, asked who and what she was? the painter replied, "Son i miei occhi."

SONNET IV.

Be frank with me, and I accept my lot;
But deal not with me as a grieving child,
Who for the loss of that which he hath not
Is by a show of kindness thus beguiled.
Raise not for me, from its enshrouded tomb,
The ghostly likeness of a hope deceased;
Nor think to cheat the darkness of my doom
By wavering doubts how far thou art released:
This dressing Pity in the garb of Love,—
This effort of the heart to *seem* the same,—
These sighs and lingerings, (which nothing prove
But that thou leav'st me with a kind of shame,)—
Remind me more, by their most vain deceit,
Of the dear loss of all which thou dost counterfeit.

SONNET V.

Because I know that there is that in me
Of which thou shouldst be proud, and not ashamed,—

Because I feel one made *thy* choice should be
  Not even by fools and slanderers rashly blame,—
Because I fear, howe'er thy soul may strive
  Against the weakness of that inward pain,
The falsehoods which my enemies contrive
  Not always seek to wound thine ear in vain,—
Therefore I sometimes weep, when I should smile,
  At all the vain frivolity and sin
Which those who know me not (yet me revile)—
  My would-be judges—cast my actions in;
But else their malice hath nor sting nor smart—
For I appeal from them, Beloved, to thine own heart!

SONNET VI.

Where the red-wine cup floweth, there art thou!
  Where luxury curtains out the evening sky;—
Triumphant Mirth sits flush'd upon thy brow,
  And ready laughter lurks within thine eye
Where the long day declineth, lone I sit,
  In idle thought, my listless hands entwined,
And, faintly smiling at remember'd wit,
  Act the scene over to my musing mind.
In my lone dreams I hear thy eloquent voice
  I see the pleased attention of the throng,

And bid my spirit in thy joy rejoice,
  Lest in love's selfishness I do thee wrong.
Ah! midst that proud and mirthful company
Send'st *thou* no wandering thought to love and me?

SONNET VII.

LIKE an enfranchised bird, who wildly springs,
  With a keen sparkle in his glancing eye
And a strong effort in his quivering wings,
  Up to the blue vault of the happy sky,—
So my enamour'd heart, so long thine own,
  At length from Love's imprisonment set free,
Goes forth into the open world alone,
  Glad and exulting in its liberty:
But like that helpless bird, (confined so long,
  His weary wings have lost all power to soar,
Who soon forgets to trill his joyous song,
  And, feebly fluttering, sinks to earth once more,—
So, from its former bonds released in vain,
My heart still feels the weight of that remember'd chain.

SONNET VIII.

TO MY BOOKS.

Silent companions of the lonely hour,
  Friends, who can never alter or forsake,
Who for inconstant roving have no power,
  And all neglect, perforce, must calmly take,—
Let me return to YOU ; this turmoil ending
  Which worldly cares have in my spirit wrought,
And, o'er your old familiar pages bending,
  Refresh my mind with many a tranquil thought,
Till, haply meeting there, from time to time,
  Fancies, the audible echo of my own,
'Twill be like hearing in a foreign clime
  My native language spoke in friendly tone,
And with a sort of welcome I shall dwell
On these, my unripe musings, told so well.

SONNET IX.

TO THE COUNTESS HELENE ZAVADOWSKY.

When our young Queen put on her rightful crown
  In Gothic Westminster's long-hallow'd walls,

The eye upon no lovelier sight looked down
  Than thou, fair Russian! Memory still recalls
The soft light of thy sapphire-color'd eyes,
  The rich twine of thy simply-braided hair,
And the low murmur of the crowd's surprise
  To see thee pass along so strangely fair.
Nor didst thou charm by looks and smiles alone,—
  Thy "broken English" had its share of grace,
For something in thy accent and thy tone
  So match'd the beauty of thy gentle face,
We seem'd to hear our old familiar words
Set to some foreign lute or harp's melodious chords!

SONNET X.

TO TAGLIONI.

Spirit of Grace, whose airy footsteps fall
  So lightly! sure the looker-on must be
Most dull of fancy who doth not recall
  Some sweet comparison to picture thee!
The white snow, drifting in its soundless showers,—
  The young bird resting on a summer-bough,—
The south wind bending down the opening flowers,—

The clear wave lifted with a gentle flow,—
Rippling and bright, advancing and retreating,
Curling around the rock its dancing spray,
Like a fair child whose kiss of gentle greeting
Woos a companion to make holiday,—
Such are the thoughts of beauty round me shed,
While pleased my eyes pursue thy light elastic tread.

SONNET XI.

THE WEAVER.

Little they think, the giddy and the vain,
Wandering at pleasure 'neath the shady trees,
While the light glossy silk or rustling train
Shines in the sun or flutters in the breeze,
How the sick weaver plies the incessant loom,
Crossing in silence the perplexing thread,
Pent in the confines of one narrow room,
Where droops complainingly his cheerless head:—
Little they think with what dull anxious eyes,
Nor by what nerveless, thin, and trembling hands,
The devious mingling of those various dyes
Where wrought to answer Luxury's commands

But the day cometh when the tired shall rest,—
Where weary Lazarus leans his head on Abraham's breast!

SONNET XII.

"Ay ojuelos verdes,
Ay los mis ojuelos,
Ay hagan los cielos
Que de mi te acuerdes!"*

Oh! crystal eyes, in which my image lay
While I was near, as in a fountain's wave
Let it not in like manner pass away
When I am gone; for I am Love's true slave,
And in *my* eyes thine image dwells enshrined,
Like one who dazzled hath beheld the sun,
So that to other beauty I am blind,
And scarce distinguish what I gaze upon:
Let it be thus with thee! By all our vows,—
By the true token-ring upon thy hand.—
Let such remembrance as my worth allows
Between thee and each bright temptation stand,—
That I, in those clear orbs, on my return,
As in the wave's green depth, my shadow may discern.

---

*See the notes to a beautiful volume of poems by Bryant, where this fragment of a Spanish ballad is given.

SONNET XIII.

TO MISS AUGUSTA COWELL.

[To whom I owe the popularity of some of my favorite ballads.]

WHEN thy light fingers touch th' obedient chords,
Which, with a gentle murmur, low respond,
Waiting the measure of the coming words
From that sweet voice, so plaintive, sad, and fond,—
Say does some winged Ariel, hovering near,
Teach thee his island music note for note,
That thou may'st copy with an echo clear
Th' enchanted symphonies that round thee float ?
Or do all Melodies, whilst thou art playing,
(Each with the offering of some chorded sound.)
On the low slanting sunbeam earthward straying,
Like meek subservient spirits wander round ;
'n Harmony's dim language asking thee
Which of them, for the hour, shall thy attendant be ?

SONNET XIV.

PRINCESS MARIE OF WIRTEMBERG.

WHITE Rose of Bourbon's branch, so early faded!
  When thou wert carried to thy silent rest,
And every brow with heavy gloom was shaded,
  And every heart with fond regret oppress'd,—
Sweet was the thought thy brother gave to him
  Who, far away on Ocean's restless wave,
Could not behold those fair eyes closed and dim
  Nor see thee laid in thy untimely grave!
And, pitying him who yet thy loss must hear,—
  Whose absent breast a later pang must feel,—
Murmur'd, with touching sadness, by thy bier,
  "Adieu for me! *Adieu for Joinville!*"
Sweet was the thought, and tender was the heart
Which thus remember'd *all* who in its love had part.*

---

* The touching anecdote is told of the youthful Duc d'Aumale, that, when the members of the royal family were bidding farewell to the sacred remains of the Princess Marie (the Prince de Joinville being then absent with his ship,) he turned with a gush of sorrow, and bid adieu, not only for himself, but in the name of his absent brother.

SONNET XV.

Nor wert thou only by thy kindred wept,—
Young mother ! gentle daughter ! cherish'd wife !
Deep in her memory France hath fondly kept
The records of thy unassuming life :
Oft shall the statue heroine* bring to mind,—
As pale it gleams beneath the light of day,
In all the thoughtful grace by thee design'd—
The worth and talent which have pass'd away !
Oft shall the old, who see thy child pass by,
Smiling and glad, despite his orphan'd lot,
Look on him with a blessing and a sigh ;
As one who suffers loss, yet feels it not,
But lifting up his innocent eyes in prayer,
Vaguely imagines Heaven,—foretaught that thou art THERE.

* The staute of Joan of Arc, designed and executed by the Princess herself.

SONNET XVI.

ON HEARING OF THE DEATH OF THE COUNTESS OF BURLINGTON.

[Inscribed, with deep and earnest sympathy, to her Mother, the Countess of Carlisle.]

SINCE in the pleasant time of opening flower,
That flower, Her life, was doom'd to fade away,—
Since Her dear loss hath shaded lovely hours,
And turn'd to mourning all the smiles of May,—
Henceforward when the warm soft breath of Spring
Bids cowslips star the meadows, thick and sweet;
When doves are in the green wood murmuring,
And children wander with delighted feet;
When, by their own rich beauty downward bent,
Soft Guelder-roses hang their tufts of snow,
And purple lilacs yield a fragrant scent,

And bright laburnum droops its yellow
bough ;—
Let that Spring-time be welcomed with a sigh,
For Her lamented sake,—who was so young to
die !

SONNET XVII.

But since, in all that brief Life's narrow scope,
No day pass'd by without some gentle deed,
Let us not "mourn like them that have no
hope,"
Though sharp the stroke,—and suddenly
decreed ;
For still, when Spring puts out her tender leaves,
And nature's beauty seems to bud in vain,
(Since then the yearning spirit doubly grieves
With fresh remembrance of unconquer'd
pain,)
Returns the precious memory of all
The grace and goodness of that creature fair,
Whom it pleased God in early days to call
From this dim world of trouble, toil, and
care,—
And seldom is such bless'd conviction given
That She we mourn on Earth is now a Saint in
Heaven !

THE END.